MEANINGFUL FUNERALS

MEANINGFUL FUNERALS

MEETING THE THEOLOGICAL AND PASTORAL CHALLENGE IN A POSTMODERN ERA

EWAN KELLY

mowbray

Published by Mowbray
A Continuum imprint
The Tower Building, 11 York Road, London SE1 7NX
80 Maiden Lane, Suite 704, New York, NY 10038

www.continuumbooks.com

Ewan Kelly has asserted his right under the Copyright, Designs and Patents Act,
1988, to be identified as the Author of this work.

British Library Cataloguing-in-Publication Data
A catalogue record for this book is available from the British Library

ISBN-10: PB: 1-9062-8614-0
ISBN-13: PB: 978-1-9062-8614-9

Typeset by Newgen Imaging Systems Pvt Ltd., Chennai, India
Printed on acid-free paper in Great Britain by Ashford Press Ltd,
Gosport, Hampshire

Contents

Preface

Since I began tentatively wrestling with existential issues raised during encounters at patients' bedsides or in parishioners' living rooms as a trainee doctor and then as a divinity student, I have increasingly believed in the need to do theology out of experience. Engaging in theological reflection based on practice involves our hearts as well as our heads. Such theology takes seriously our feelings, physicality and sexuality as well as rationality. Moreover, as a Church of Scotland minister working in parish, hospital, hospice and academic contexts over the past 15 years applying theology developed solely within the academy to particular situations of crisis or need has seemed increasingly irrelevant. As part of my journey to explore the implications of an inductive approach to doing pastoral theology I have written this book. It comes out of the desire not just to improve ritual practice as part of the church's care of the bereaved but also to reflect theologically on the experience of what it means to share in the construction and performance of funerals with those who grieve. Such theologising is important in informing the future approach to, and practice of, what I believe has become the most significant and relevant function the church is perceived to have within twenty-first century Western society – helping individuals, families and communities, both local and global, ritually mark the lives and deaths of significant others.

Engaging in pastoral theology in such a manner requires practice to reflect on. For the purposes of this book, I have utilised the bereavement experiences lived through by a small cohort of parents whose babies have died *in-utero* to inform my reflections. These parents were supported by former hospital chaplaincy colleagues who helped facilitate the co-construction and performance of relevant funerals for their babies. Their stories were gathered through qualitative interviewing. Furthermore, I have also utilised case studies from my own practice of helping the bereaved to co-author and share in the funeral for their loved one within the context of my work as a hospice chaplain.[1]

Numerous people have helped this book to come to fruition. The Health Department of the Chief Scientist Office (CSO) of the Scottish Government and the Hope Trust enabled my research with bereaved parents to be financed.

Former colleagues within the multidisciplinary team at the Royal Infirmary of Edinburgh, often unknowingly, were a great source of encouragement and inspiration through their practice, expertise and humanity. I owe a great deal to the midwives, neonatal nurses and doctors with whom I worked and from whom I gained much. The management team in the Simpson as well the Research and Development Team in the Royal Infirmary of Edinburgh were nothing but generous in their giving of time and support. My friends and former colleagues, Sandy Young, Iain Telfer, Anne Mulligan and Gordon Muchall, in the Department of Spiritual Care could not have been more understanding, encouraging and patient. Fiona Allan and Grace Dobie gave valuable administrative and secretarial support.

Current colleagues in St Columba's Hospice continue to offer friendship, genuine openness to collaborative holistic care, compassion and the sense of humour required to work both in palliative care and with me. Fred Benton has given me the permission to take time and space to write and Brian Hilsley,

---

1   All those who attend a funeral are active participants. It is important that the chief mourners have control over the extent to which they actively participate and are comfortable with the level of their involvement. This may involve choosing particular clothes to wear, choosing flowers to offer, singing hymns, carrying the coffin, standing at the crematorium door to receive condolences or making a donation to a retiring collection. In some instances, family member(s) may wish to share memories of their loved during the funeral, read from scripture or a poem, sing or play an instrument or invite friends to do so on their behalf.

Stewart McPherson and John Tait provided chaplaincy cover when I was ensconced at a laptop.

Numerous University of Edinburgh colleagues, within and outwith the School of Divinity, have freely offered their advice, guidance and listening ears. I owe a great deal to Duncan Forrester, William Storrar and David Lyall, in particular, as mentors, colleagues and friends. David read various drafts of the text and helped the development of otherwise vague notions. It is not only the depth of his insights that are appreciated but the manner in which they were shared.

I am grateful to the parents who shared their stories and to the patients and their bereaved loved ones with whom I have worked with over the years. The dying and the bereaved are our teachers. They are also theologians and pastoral commentators of great profundity.

The editorial and publishing team at Continuum have been immeasurably supportive and patient. Thanks to Fiona Murphy for believing in this project and to Thomas Kraft and Dominic Mattos for their help ensuring I completed it. I am also grateful to Murali and his colleagues at Newgen Imaging Systems for their courteous and efficient provision of copyediting, typesetting and proofreading.

Lastly, to my family and friends (alive and dead) who share lasting, continuing bonds with me, shape me and inform me, love me no matter what and construct and share rituals with me – my ongoing gratitude.

Acknowledgements

I would like to acknowledge the following works:

Alan Horner, extract from 'Vulnerability' from *A Picture with the Paint Still Wet* (Revaph Publications, 2005), reprinted with permission of Margaret Horner.

Anne Stevenson, *Poems 1955–2005* (Bloodaxe Books, 2005).

Anonymous, 'Act of Farewell', reprinted with permission of the Stillbirth and Neonatal Society (SANDS).

Iain Crighton Smith, extract from 'On Looking at the Dead' from *Collected Poems* (Carcanet Press, 1995).

Michael Rosen, extract from 'Don't Tell Me I Mourn Too Much' from *Carrying the Elephant* (Penguin, 2002).

Norman MacCaig, extract from 'Praise of a Man' from *Poems of Norman MacCaig* (Polygon, an imprint of Birlinn Ltd. www.birlinn.co.uk<outbind://176/www.birlinn.co.uk, 2005).

Roger McGough, 'I Am Not Sleeping' from *Selected Poems* (Penguin, 2006), reprinted with permission of PFD (www.pfd.co.uk) on behalf of Roger McGough.

Roger McGough, 'Sad Music' from *Everyday Eclipses* (Penguin, 2002), reprinted with permission of PFD (www.pfd.co.uk) on behalf of Roger McGough.

Susan Wallbank, 'Death Makes Philosophers of Us All' from *All in the End is Harvest* (DLT/Cruse, 1984).

Sydney Carter, extract from '*The Good Boy*' from *The Two-way Clock* (Stainer and Bell Ltd, 1974).

William Soutar, extract from 'Song' from *Poems of William Soutar: A New Selection.* (Sottish Academic Press, 188), reprinted with permission of the Trustees of the National Library of Scotland.

1

Introduction

This book has evolved from reflection on the practice of church representatives seeking to co-create and share in funerals with the bereaved. It aims to stimulate practitioners to reflect theologically and practically on how they approach funeral construction and performance. As part of the church's care of the bereaved, it may also encourage students to engage with theological, psychological, social and practical issues relating to funerals and how they are constructed. In essence, this book is an attempt to provide a constructive response to the following:

> There appears to be a general consensus in the area that the rituals of the past must be helpful to people who have been bereaved but it remains undemonstrated exactly how such rituals might be rehabilitated in order to fit contemporary, complex and secular societies. (Littlewood 1993, 78)

Moreover, it is hoped that this book will provoke some thought on the priorities of those ministering in parish settings, in an era where contact with people who are not actively involved in the church is increasingly often restricted to those seeking help with ritual marking of their life and death or that of a loved one. All too often such 'parish funerals' are seen as a burden rather than opportunity to share God's love, another chore to squeeze into an already full diary rather than a priority which requires time, creativity and attentiveness of the highest quality.

What is offered in these pages is the thesis that church representatives, in helping to facilitate the process of co-constructing the ritual marking of a particular life and death, have a significant therapeutic role in helping people to deal with their grief. The therapeutic effect of enabling the bereaved to co-author meaningful funerals for a significant other which responds to their particular needs, experience, beliefs and feelings will be described with reference to qualitative research undertaken with bereaved parents. However, in our postmodern Western world, where the majority of people are unfamiliar with the Christian metanarrative and its language and symbolism, does helping to create and share in such funerals undermine the church representative's theological integrity? This and other questions which arise when practice is allowed to shape and influence theology will be addressed. Such an approach to doing pastoral theology is not new. In describing the relationship between liturgy and pastoral care, Elaine Graham, though writing about the expression of sexuality in both, says something highly pertinent about the failings of a set liturgical response to the needs of the bereaved within a funeral context. She describes – 'the dislocation between liturgy and pastoral care; the former appearing sanitised, esoteric and irrelevant, the latter dealing with the nitty-gritty of human need, the failures and triumphs' (Graham 2000, 95–6).

Hence, Graham stresses that liturgical reform develops from reflection on pastoral practice. Her thesis resonates with the central concepts proposed in this book. However, what is proposed here goes further for it will be suggested that though the resources offered to the bereaved by a Christian ritual leader during the process of the co-construction of a funeral may be informed by the liturgy of her religious tradition, they should not be imposed. It is suggested that each individual ritual marking the life and death of a particular human being should be unique. In other words, the funeral should evolve out of the specific needs, beliefs, feelings and experiences of the bereaved and their deceased loved one as they are heard and interpreted by the representative of the Christian community invited to facilitate the creation of the ritual and to share in its performance.

This is not to deny the identity, beliefs and actions of the carer, for her story will not only inform what is co-constructed but it is also to enable ritual to be relevant, grounded and owned by those who participate in it. 'For the liturgy to be effective it needs to articulate and speak to the experience of those who take part in it, word and symbol' (Stuart 1992, 11). This requires honesty, vulnerability and a willingness by the ritual leader to begin where the bereaved are and not where they are assumed to be. It means the church representative needs to listen to the story of the bereaved and acknowledge the influence of her own story on the developing pastoral relationship and what is being co-constructed.

This book is not a liturgical treatise, nor even an exposition of how pastoral practice should shape the creation of liturgies to be utilised, even adapted, in certain circumstances. It is about doing theology following reflection on, and research into, practice and that theology informing future practice with particular individuals and families. Therefore, the intention is not to create and offer specific liturgical texts to impose from above onto particular circumstances or family cultures. What is offered are theological reflections on working with, and learning from, the bereaved while seeking to meet their needs through the co-creation of, and shared participation in, funerals. It is not only the bereaved who can benefit from interaction with a church representative but also the ritual leader and, thus, the church she represents may learn more about how to care, how to be human and in doing so learn more about God.

The approach to creating meaningful funerals proposed in the following pages takes seriously what it is to be bereaved in a postmodern context where the majority of the population derive their sense of meaning and understanding of their experience from a plethora of worldviews, beliefs and spiritual practices. Moreover, such a methodology recognises the lack of intimate knowledge of death and the ritual associated with it currently prevalent in the Western world. This book also suggests that if the ritual practice of church representatives is to take seriously contemporary models of grieving (shaped by the research and reflections of mental health practitioners and sociologists) then it is significant for the well-being of the bereaved that they are actively involved in the authorship of funerals for their deceased loved one. There is, as the sociologist Tony Walter (1999) points out, a need for the bereaved in their vulnerability and anxiety to know that their feelings are normal and appropriate. The lack of cultural norms as to how to deal with death in an urban postmodern society has created a need for the availability of some external points of reference against which the bereaved may gauge their own experience, feelings and behaviour. Walter suggests that such regulation of grief is currently done by a value system or framework which is now outdated for many bereaved people – traditional, prescribed religious funerals which may add to, instead of lessening, their feelings of disorientation and lack of control. This book suggests that the church still has much to offer the bereaved and society in general not just in creatively enabling the bereaved to co-author and share in meaningful funerals but also in providing a more relevant way in which grief may be sensitively normalised.

To ensure that the term 'meaningful funeral' does not just remain an abstract term, I will outline below two funerals which involved co-construction between bereaved families and myself. The actual process of how funerals may be co-constructed is described more fully in Chapter 5.

The first example is that of a stillborn baby whose young mother had a church upbringing but was now no longer affiliated with a local congregation and whose father had no knowledge of the Christian tradition whatsoever. As a hospital chaplain I first met Jonathan and Haley in labour ward when they asked for help and information regarding having a funeral for their baby (they did not want a separate blessing or naming ritual). During our first meeting I met their baby, Robert, listened to as much of their story as they felt able to share, gave them some practical information (the midwife had already given them written information) about making funeral arrangements and said that I would meet with them in the next few days, when they felt ready, to talk further. Haley's mother joined us at the end of our conversation and expressed grave doubts about the ability of her teenage daughter, especially in such a distressed state, to participate in a process to help create an appropriate funeral for Robert. Haley, however, was insistent that she want to help plan something special for her son. The next day, at their request, before Jonathan and Haley left the hospital, I gave them some resources, sacred and secular, which other bereaved parents had utilised during their baby's funeral and emphasised that they had as much time as they needed before we made any decisions about the ritual. The three of us met together twice in Haley's mother's house, where the couple were living, before Robert's cremation. The couple asked three friends to provide musical accompaniment for the singing during the service and had selected CD tracks to be played. Haley and Jonathan chose the funeral content in discussion with me and sought advice regarding the service's order. Jonathan's brother then created and printed out an order of service for his nephew, a copy of which was handed to every mourner by Haley's cousins at the crematorium door. What the young couple helped to construct during the week following their baby's stillbirth is as follows:

While the mourners gathered in the crematorium (over a hundred of them, including family, college and school friends, teachers and a couple of members of staff from the maternity unit) a CD of the rap artist Puff Daddy singing 'I'll Be Missing You' (Money 1997) was played.[1]

Jonathan carried his son's coffin into the crematorium accompanied by Haley who carried a posy of forget-me-nots picked from her mother's garden and a framed photograph of herself and Jonathan with Robert (these were placed in front of the catafalque).

---

1 A rap song exploring grief, including the pain of broken physical bonds and the acute sense of loss felt when an individual can no longer pray, as before a bereavement, for the deceased's health and well-being in this life.

I welcomed everyone to the funeral and said that though we did not all have the opportunity to meet Robert in person we all were touched by his life and death. We had all waited expectantly for his arrival and shared hopes and dreams with his mum and dad for him and for the three of them. We also may have seen photographs of Robert or heard what a beautiful baby he was – dark haired like his dad with the button nose of his mum. We were all sad and perplexed at the death of Robert before he had the chance to enjoy life but we were also there with Jonathan and Haley to give thanks for the love, joy and hope that Robert had brought into their lives and into the lives of all who cared for them.

Together we then all sang 'We cannot care for you the way we wanted' (Bell 2005).

I read a short reflection written by Jonathan and Haley about Robert, their relationship with him and their thoughts and feelings surrounding his death.

Haley's aunt read:

> Can a woman forget the infant at her breast,
> or a mother the child of her womb?
> But should even these forget,
> I shall never forget you.
> I have inscribed you on the palms of
> my hands.
>
> (Isaiah 49:15–16a)

A friend of Jonathan's read an extract from 'To the immortal Memory and Friendship of that Noble Pair, Sir Lucius Cary and Sir Henry Morison' by Ben Jonson (cited by Dominica 1997, 81) which contains the lines:

> In small proportions we just beauty see,
> And short measures life may perfect be.

Together as we stood, the whole congregation said these words of farewell:

Child of my flesh
bone of my bone
wherever you go, I will go,
wherever you live, I will live.
As you go into the mystery of life before us
may you be at peace.
That in God's good time
we may be together in peace.
(Stillbirth and Neonatal Death Society cited
by Dominica 1997, 58)

Brahm's Lullaby was then quietly played by the instrumentalists. Prayers of lament and thanksgiving and prayers for the bereaved were said. The final hymn: 'Fleetingly known, yet ever remembered' (Stillbirth and Neonatal Death Society cited by Dominica 1997, 113) was sung to the tune 'Bunessan'.

I ended the funeral with a short benediction.

As the congregation left the chapel Bob Dylan's (1973) song 'Forever Young' was played.

Following the funeral over 50 friends and relatives gathered in Haley's mother's home where music was played and listened to and stories about Jonathan, Haley and Robert were shared over refreshments.

An example of a co-constructed non-religious funeral is one in which I shared for Bruce, a 40- year-old Scottish civil servant, who died in the hospice where I work. Bruce was single and had a wide circle of friends, many of whom shared his passion for the outdoors and for his country's cultural and political heritage. He had been very involved in the piping and folk music world and enjoyed watching sport. Together with his two sisters and his parents, as well as respecting the wishes of Bruce, the following funeral was co-authored:

A pibroch (lament) was played on the bagpipes (by a close friend) as Bruce was carried into the crematorium by his brothers-in-law and another two friends.

I welcomed everyone to the funeral and acknowledged the tragedy and injustice of Bruce's death at such a comparatively young age. However, I added that Bruce had touched all of our lives in his own incorrigible way, he had left us all with a myriad of memories and stories to share of life lived with him. I invited everyone to remember Bruce in their own particular way as we listened to the tune 'Highland Cathedral' on the pipes (this tune was especially pertinent as Bruce loved to watch Scotland play rugby at Murrayfield and in recent years it has been played as the players run onto the pitch prior to the start of a game).

Bruce's closest friend then shared some of his reflections on Bruce's life.

Amazing Grace (words by Newton and tune 'New Britain' arranged by Bell 2005) was then played on the pipes while we all listened and those of us familiar with the words reflected on them.[2]

Verses from 1 Corinthians 13 were then read as the family felt the words reflected what Bruce was essentially about – loving and encouraging others to utilise their musical talents and administrative and political skills as best they could and the fact that their love for him had brought a disparate range of friends and family together for the funeral.

A poem entitled 'Epitaph on My Own Friend' from the pen of Scotland's national bard, Robert Burns (cited by MacGregor 2005, 39) was then read. It contains the following lines:

> If there's another world, he lives in bliss:
> If there is none, he made the best of this.

---

2 While respecting Bruce's beliefs and his request to have a non-religious funeral, his mother, who was loosely affiliated to her local church, wanted some reference to the hope that faith in a loving, merciful God can offer during the service. In discussing this with her and the rest of the family, listening to Amazing Grace played on the pipes was an acceptable compromise – Bruce's sisters felt that he would have been comfortable with what had been agreed upon (including the biblical reading from 1 Corinthians 13 that followed).

No words were spoken as family and friends stood to acknowledge their last farewell to Bruce while the crematorium's curtains were drawn separating them from his coffin but the gentle tune 'Dream Angus' (Angus was Bruce's family name) was played on the Lowland pipes. This was the tune Bruce's mother had hummed to all her children before they fell asleep as children and Bruce had done likewise with his nieces and nephews.

We continued to stand in the quiet after the lilt of the pipes had drifted away paying our respects to Bruce and in the quiet, those gathered had the opportunity to pray or to have their own thoughts.

Finally, we sung together Burns's most famous song – 'Auld Lang Syne', people joining hands with their neighbours, as is traditional, at the appropriate point in the song.

As a way of marking of the end of the funeral, I said:

> As you go from this place,
> go gently,
> go lightly,
> and may the many memories of Bruce you carry with you,
> in time, give you comfort and hope for the journey ahead.

A retiring collection took place for the hospice and Bruce's family invited all present to a local hotel, a favourite haunt of Bruce's, where refreshments and reminisces were shared as the Lowland pipes, the fiddles and guitars played late into the evening.

Before outlining how the life and death of an individual (or indeed several persons) may be marked by a process of ritualisation, the context in which funerals and their allied informal rituals take place in will be described in the following three chapters.

2

The Postmodern Context and the Need for Ritual Following Death

Postmodern Society

Before beginning to explore how meaningful funerals may be constructed which meet the specific needs of a particular family and enable a church representative supporting them to maintain theological integrity, it is important to outline something of the wider context in which they meet. A description of predominant contemporary Western culture may help deepen our understanding of some of the worldviews and expectations that the bereaved bring to the planning and construction of the funerals of their loved ones.

As David Lyall (1999, 8) a pastoral theologian much engaged with how the church may offer relevant pastoral care in the twenty-first century admits, it is difficult to pin down what postmodernism actually is. In attempting to contextualise his theological reflections on pastoral practice he quotes Smart (1993, 12):

> postmodernity as a contemporary social, cultural and political condition. Postmodernity as a form of life, a form of reflection upon and a response to the accumulating signs of the limits and limitations of modernity.

Modernity is commonly understood as an epoch in Western history which was based on the rationality of post-Newtonian science and the ideas of the seventeenth- and eighteenth-century Enlightenment. During this period, there was an unquestioning belief in science, reason, education and the inevitability of progress as well as a steady marginalisation and privatisation of faith. Bauman (1991) importantly highlights that the influence of modernity has not ceased because we have entered a seemingly different cultural and philosophical milieu. Remnants of modernity undoubtedly continue to influence contemporary culture as shall be further explored later in this chapter in relation to ritual need.

Our predominantly postmodern Western world is a confusing and contradictory place to inhabit, especially at times of crisis such as bereavement; a variety of understandings and worldviews compete for our attention and response. There are few, if any, shared cultural norms or certainties to guide and inform us, especially in periods of transition and bewilderment.

Paul Ballard (2005, 48) outlines three hallmarks of postmodern culture:

- the collapse of metanarratives or common cultural consensus,
- the autonomy of the individual which is taken to mean that one carves out one's own world of meaning,
- a sharp divide between the public and the private.

These three central components offer a structure around which a description of present day society may be made.

The Collapse of Metanarratives or Common Cultural Consensus

Postmodern philosophy hinges on dogged scepticism of given overriding 'legitimizing "master narratives"' (Butler 2002, 13) which in past eras have greatly influenced individual and societal values, worldviews and practices. In a postmodern world not only is the authenticity of the grand narrative expounded by preachers and contextualised by theologians called into question but so too are those formulated and rehearsed by scientists, historians and sociologists. In our era of multitudinous worldviews such arguments:

> are to be seen as no more than quasi narratives which compete with all the others for acceptance. They have no unique or reliable fit to the world, no certain correspondence with reality. They are just another form of fiction. (Butler 2002, 15)

In the past, the Christian faith within the Western world was perceived, especially by many within the church, as being based on objective truths and having a special place within a spectrum of faith. However, currently:

> the church interfaces with a world which sees it simply as another voice among voices. . . . Relativism . . . has placed Christianity, philosophically and theoretically, on the same basis as all other belief systems. (Irvine 1997, 59)

In the postmodern world, the Christian story is viewed as one of a plethora of narratives offering a variety of relative truths from which an individual can select and form their own subjective truths (Page 2000). For many who do affiliate themselves with the Christian tradition there are also fewer absolutes. This is of particular relevance in the consideration of the potential beliefs of the dying and the bereaved. Former hospice chaplain Derek Murray (2002, 30) states:

> The stern-sounding beliefs of earlier centuries have broken down in our times, and been succeeded by a mixture of dogmatic doubt and vague yearnings. It seems to be assumed that God is obliged 'by Gospel truth and Gospel law' to accept everyone of goodwill and that the old doctrines of salvation and resurrection are relics of a past age. Far from people being terrified to die because of fear

of what awaits them they often express a great confidence
in a better time coming, and their fears are much more
immediate. They express fear of dying, not of death itself. ✗

One measure of the reduction of influence of the Christian
metanarrative in Western society is to note the number of
people attending church and the beliefs of a given population.

In Britain, for example, church attendance has declined
from 19 per cent in 1903 to 15 per cent in 1951, to 12 per
cent in 1979, to 10 per cent in 1989 and to an estimated 8
per cent in 2000 (Wraight and Brierley 1999, 26 cited by
Woodhead et al. [2003, 4]).

Sociologist Steve Bruce (2003, 55 citing Opinion Research
Business 2000), who has written and researched widely in the
field of secularisation in Britain, feels:

there is plenty of evidence that Christian beliefs are
declining behind, but in step with, institutional decline. In
the 1950s, 43 per cent of the population said they believed
in a personal God. In the 1990s, the figure was 31 per cent.
In a May 2000 survey, it was 26 per cent.

For Callum Brown (2001), secularisation in Britain is not
just about decline in religious adherence or church attendance
but also about how Christianity is no longer the frame of reference by which people construct their social and moral selves;
their sense of identity. In contemporary society, Christianity has
markedly less influence on the cultural norms or values by which
people lead their lives than it had in previous generations.

Kay Hunt conducted a series of qualitative interviews with
people in the Nottingham area of England who did not go to
church. She concluded from her research findings that few
people had any significant knowledge of the Christian faith
and did not consider themselves religious. However, she did

find that they had beliefs 'in "something"' (Hunt 2003, 164), that 'something' being difficult to articulate as the traditional language of Christian orthodoxy was not familiar to people and, thus, irrelevant.

Those who live in the Western world not only inhabit a culture of relativism and declining Christian influence but also live in a pluralistic matrix of an increasing diversity of religions and worldviews. However, though the ethnic population of Britain is gradually becoming more varied the number of people who are affiliated with religions other than Christianity is still relatively small. In answer to a voluntary question relating to religious affiliation 72 per cent of the population dentified themselves as Christian, 15 per cent voiced no sense of attachment to any particular faith, 5 per cent identified themselves with other faith communities and 8 per cent chose not to answer the question (Cobb 2005 citing the 2001 Census in the United Kingdom). From these figures, it can be observed that the majority of those affiliating themselves with the Christian tradition in Britain either are 'cultural' Christians or have some Christian beliefs but do not wish to actively belong to a local faith community.

Any interest in diversity, such that there is, is not an urge to discover a new way of living or set of beliefs and values argues Bauman (1991). It is an armchair activity rather than a participatory one, encouraged by the voyeuristic programmes shown on television. Such 'market-promoted tolerance does not lead to solidarity: it fragments, instead of uniting' (Bauman 1991, 274). This ambivalence towards the range of worldviews, beliefs and values which may inform an individual's perceptions exemplifies the postmodern condition.

The Autonomy of the Individual – Carving Out One's Own World of Meaning

Paul Heelas and Linda Woodhead (2005, 2) have developed the concept that in recent years Western society has undergone what Taylor (1991, 26) calls 'the massive subjective turn of modern culture'. Their thesis is that rather than referring to external authorities, such as religious traditions and scriptures and inherited cultural and familial norms as the overarching framework within which to construct and reconstruct beliefs, attitudes and ethical perspectives, individuals in our postmodern world are increasingly becoming more attentive to their own experiences, feelings and perceived need. These have become the main point of reference for many, as is exemplified in Leonard Cohen's (2003, 83) poem 'Dear Diary', in which he admits his diary, a personal interpretation of his interactions, thoughts and feelings, is 'more sublime' to him than any canonical script. Heelas and Woodhead (2005, 3) describe such a shift in attitude.

> The subjective turn is thus a turn away from 'life–as' (life lived as dutiful wife, father, husband, strong leader, self–made man etc) to 'subjective–life' (life lived in deep connection with the unique experiences of my self–in–relation).

Furthermore, they deduce from their research into the worshiping and reflexive habits of the population of Kendal in England that those institutions, including churches, which facilitate connection with only higher or external authorities are out of step with prevailing culture. Those activities, including styles of worship, which enable individuals to meditate on, and search for meaning in, their own experience (in relation to others and the wider world) are becoming increasingly popular. Hence, the growing numbers of people who make regular time for yoga or one of an array of holistic therapies or who attend worship with an emphasis on ritual and liturgy, for example, in cathedrals.

In our postChristian society, formalised religion is less influential in shaping peoples' worldviews and behaviour as it once was. However, there remains an interest in the transcendent and that which may give meaning and purpose to life.

In methods ranging from New Age to Ignatian, people are searching for personal meaning. There is a free market in religion, and in this 'pick and mix' culture, people are putting together their own packages, finding a religious or spiritual stance which makes sense from their own perspectives shaped by the stories of their own lives. (Lyall 1999, 9)

What postmodernism makes legitimate is individual processing of, and reflection on, received ideas, beliefs and values in relation to our own particular story. In present day Western society, we have permission to be our own person and in relation to matters of belief to do our own theology and not simply absorb and accept that which is handed on to us. Gergen (1991, 111 cited by hospital chaplain Leon Sims [1998, 251]) postulates that this is an ongoing process throughout life:

we are dealing with the full-scale abandonment of the concept of objective truth ... Under postmodern conditions, persons exist in a state of conscious construction and reconstruction ... Each reality of self gives way to reflexive questioning, irony, and ultimately the playful probing of another reality.

Many people turn to music as means of relaxing and transcending the material and temporal aspect of life. During Christmas 2005, BBC Radio 3 played the complete works of Bach uninterrupted for ten days. John Eliot Gardiner, one of the world's foremost interpreters of Bach's music was interviewed by Alan Rusbridger (2005, 13) at the time of the Bach radio celebrations. The Archbishop of Canterbury, who was involved in presenting some of the music, posed the question whether Bach's sacred music was interpreted differently by Christians and non-Christians. In this context, Rusbridger enquired of Gardiner whether he was a Christian. Gardiner's response was truly postmodern:

At the moment I truly perform the music I am a Christian, yes. Culturally, yes. Doctrinally and theologically, no.

I have to subscribe at the moment of performing, even preparing. And I'm acutely aware there's another realm of existence out there. But do I subscribe to the whole catechism? No, of course I don't. I can't. (Rusbridger 2005, 13)

Gardiner selects what he personally finds helpful and life enhancing for him from the Christian tradition and rejects that which he considers irrational and irrelevant. There is resonance with Gardiner's approach to belief for those who are confessing Christians – few, if any, accept all of their particular tradition's orthodoxies or creeds. As the title of a recent book by Scottish practical theologian Duncan Forrester, '*Unsystematic Theology*', suggests the theology any church member develops is piecemeal, informed by fragments gathered from received wisdom shared in worship, the classroom or at home, through reading the Bible and other thought-provoking texts and reflection on our human experience; wholesale deference to the authority of the church's orthodox teaching or official moral stances by those who are influenced by the Christian narrative, whether they are active in communities of faith or not, is increasingly uncommon in our postmodern world, if it ever was the norm.

Sharp Divide between the Public and the Private

In postmodern culture not only are individuals creating their own particular worldviews and participating in spiritual practices selected from a variety of religious and non-religious sources, they are tending to do so on their own rather than communally. George Hunsberger suggests that in his home country of the United States secularisation is not so much about a reduction in religious belief but a privatisation of those beliefs and their expression. What has gradually occurred in this generation is a relocation of religion from the public to private domain.[1] Hay and Hunt (2000, 26) suggest from their research in Nottingham into the belief systems of people who don't go to church that God has been privatised into 'a household god'– useful for looking after kith and kin in times of crisis:

> Traditional monotheism is still the natural religious assumption for the ordinary person in the street, but as a practical belief the idea has been watered down to mean not much more than that God will intervene if my relatives or I get into difficulty.

In the Western world in recent years there has been 'the passage from traditional forms of religion to more personal and individual expressions of what is called "spirituality".' (The Catholic Communications Office, 2003, 1 cited by Heelas and Woodhead 2005, 1).

There is what Heelas and Woodhead (2005) a 'concurrent secularisation and sacralisation' of contemporary British society. As we leave the modern period dominated by rationality and science, individuals are rediscovering a sense of the sacred or transcendent in life and in their living. However, people are no longer drawn to traditional or communal means of seeking or expressing the otherness found within themselves, in their relationships or beyond human endeavour. Tacey (2004, 39) comments of this phenomenon:

> While only a tiny minority of people continue to practice formal religion in the developing world, huge numbers are keenly pursuing spirituality and individual pathways to sacred meaning.

Not only are they doing so but many are condemning in their attitude to 'external authorities'. The perceived hierarchical, limited and limiting practices and doctrines of organised

---

1 Taken from a lecture delivered by George Hunsberger in the School of Divinity, University of Edinburgh 5 May 2003.

religion in comparison with the subjective possibilities of spirituality are articulated by the American human rights activist Gloria Steinham (2005, 28):

> I hope that spirituality overwhelms religion. I say this because spirituality links, religion ranks; spirituality sees God in all living things, religion rations out God to some more than others; spirituality celebrates life, religion celebrates life after death. I hope we choose self-authority over hierarchy.

Death in the Postmodern World

There are two concurrent, yet very different, approaches to dealing with death in our postmodern culture.

The Denial of Death

The manner in which much of contemporary society deals with death not only reflects current discomfort with death as part of life but helps perpetuate the myth that mortality is an event which human beings do not need to confront, attempt to own nor live life within its framework. In Western society, the majority of people still find the subject of death taboo (National Council for Palliative Care, 2005). Death has become increasingly privatised and sanitised; an event which occurs at arms length and out of sight of the majority. Incongruently, deaths thousands of miles away are brought into our front rooms by technology, yet in reality death seldom occurs upstairs or next door. Death has become an event we experience second hand on screen or in our newspapers. The fact that three generation households are no longer commonplace, families (and communities) are more fractured and disparate and individuals are more likely to be hospitalised during their final illness means that for most exposure to death and dying, especially in the first half of their lifetime, is the exception rather than the norm

(National Council for Palliative Care, 2005). Walter (1990, 33) offers a slightly different perspective:

> death is *not* very much present today: it is irrelevant rather than repressed, hidden rather than forbidden. If the bereaved person finds others embarrassed, crossing to the other side of the street, I suspect it is not so much because they dare not, cannot, confront death, but because they have had very little practice at it, do not know what to do, are scared of saying the wrong thing.

In the Western world the majority of people die in healthcare institutions rather than in their own home, for example, in the United Kingdom 60 per cent of deaths occur in hospital (Clark 2002) and in the United States 80 per cent do so (McCullough 1998). In England and Wales only one in five people die at home (Higginson and Addington–Hall 2002).[2] Death, therefore, in the postmodern world is no longer a communal event. Bouwsma (1998, 189–90), a European cultural historian, comments of death in Western culture:

> In traditional representations of death beds . . . the dying are surrounded by families, friends and clergy, constituting a close and supportive community – rather than by medical professionals and machines. This larger community, in our increasingly mobile and atomised (and secular)[3] society, has now in many cases disappeared.

Karen Armstrong (2006a, 32), a historian with an interest in world religions, reflects on her mother's slow wait for death while in hospital:

> We have banished death, a disturbing reminder of our ultimate impotence, from modern society. Old people no

---

2 The rest die in nursing and residential homes and hospices, as well as in hospital.

3 My words in parentheses.

longer receive the respect they enjoyed in more traditional civilisations. Instead we push them out of sight into
residential care. Death happens off-stage in hospices and
nursing homes. And now, it seems, death is even becoming taboo in our hospitals; when we go to hospital we are
meant to get better and meet government targets; we
are not supposed to die there anymore.

For Bauman (1991), the modern era sought through rational
endeavour to overcome the forces of nature and the ambiguity
of human experiences. Disease and the anxieties and suffering
it led to was to be eradicated. Death, therefore, was not only a
failure but also something which fundamentally confronted the
modern worldview. Medical sociologist David Clark (2002,
905) reminds us that since Ivan Illich launched his now famous
treatise on the 'medicalisation' of death, Western healthcare has
struggled to eradicate the continuing dominant attitude to
death as 'something to be resisted, postponed or avoided'.

It is not just within the world of medicine that there are sure
signs that death makes contemporary Western culture uncomfortable. The deceased seldom return to their home prior to
their funeral, being kept in the care of the funeral director after
being removed from their place of death. Very few families are
now involved in the final washing and dressing of their deceased
loved one in preparation for burial or cremation; such 'last
offices' are performed by nurses in hospitals or hospices or by
the funeral director. Funeral directors offer embalming or
'treatment of the deceased's body' to avoid odours or significant post-mortem changes. The funeral director commonly
now communicates with crematoria or cemetery staff and the
ritual leader on behalf of the bereaved to arrange a time and
place for a funeral. The placing of a newspaper announcement
to publicly acknowledge the death of an individual is also
organised by the same. Caring professionals now perform roles
that families traditionally did in the past. We are in danger of
disempowering the bereaved, reducing and sanitising their

exposure to death and, thus, lessening to some degree the opportunity to confront their own mortality, as well as the death of their loved one.

Those who perform funerals, informed by Christian theology and secular ideals, can also stand accused of attempting to dumb down the reality and finality of death. Church representatives may place an emphasis on resurrection and celebration when they perform funerals to the seeming detriment of the significance of death and the pain of bereavement. Popular poems or pieces of prose read at funerals overtly deny the death event and its impact on mourners. For example, the oft-read poem 'Do not stand at my grave and weep' (cited by Astley 2003, 38) includes the stanza:

> When you awaken in the morning's hush
> I am the swift uplifting rush
> Of quiet birds in a circled flight.
> I am the soft stars that shine at night.
> Do not stand at my grave and cry;
> I am not there. I did not die.

The Revival of Death[4]

As well as the seemingly strong urge within contemporary society to marginalise death from the experience and impact of death, there has been born a counterculture which seeks otherwise. Iain Crighton-Smith (2005, 24–5) in his poem 'On Looking at the Dead' encapsulates beautifully the paradox of the harsh reality of death, yet the significance of it to life:

> a brutal thing where no chimeras are
>
> nor purple colours nor a gleam of silk
> nor any embroideries eastern or the rest

---

4   Taken from the title of Tony Walter's (1994) book.

but unavoidable beyond your choice
and therefore central and of major price.

For Crighton-Smith and for many in our postmodern world, death is too important an event for individuals, families and communities to be kept at arms length, leaving it to the caring professionals to deal with or observed merely through the filter of media technology.

From the late 1960s onwards emerged a group of increasingly influential of clinicians who raised the profile of death and dying within academic and caring professional circles, most famously Elisabeth Kubler-Ross. She enabled the psychological experiences of the dying to be heard and subsequently wrote widely on death and dying (Lawbaugh 2005). Steadily over the past 30 years death and dying has become an increasingly prevalent subject researched, written about and taught in the spheres of medicine, psychology, sociology and pastoral theology. The advent of palliative care and the hospice movement has undoubtedly played a significant role in raising the profile of the needs of the dying and the bereaved. There are other signs within our society that some do wish to return death to be part of life and no longer hold it at arms length. Guidebooks on preparing for death and dying and their associated rituals are more readily available, if not yet on the bestseller list.[5] Many individuals make clear their wishes in their wills, not just for the financial redistribution of their assets but also for their funeral and their final resting place. Increasingly, people want funerals to mark their unique life or the life of their loved one in a manner relevant to their particular story. They want to do it their way, 'not the undertakers' way, or the crematorium's way, or the religious way' (Walter 1994, 33).

Murray (2002, 32) sums up well the two opposing yet prevalent attitudes towards death in the Western world, one seeking

---

5   For example, *The Natural Death Handbook* (Wienrich, S. and Speyer, J. [eds] 2003) is now on its fourth edition since its initial publication in 1993.

to keep death at arm's length and the other accepting its inevitability and impact:

> Despite the privatisation of death, it remains firmly in the centre of human experience. It can be argued that we have become more sensitive to its terrors and more able to counsel the dying and the bereaved at the same time as death itself has left home and disappeared into hospitals.

Ritual Need in a Postmodern World

With the Demise of the Judeo-Christian, metanarrative Western culture is thus bereft of a shared means by which to express our search for meaning and purpose in the face of human mortality. There is no longer a common language or symbolism by which we can express our longings, fears and helplessness in relation to the meeting of the mysteries that are life and death. Society no longer has an overarching framework within which there can be corporate exploration of questions of suffering and injustice. There is yearning within the Western world to fill this void, particularly when dealing with the impact of significant loss.

Ritual following personal, familial, communal, national and global tragedy which seeks to respond to people's need to search for meaning and purpose that uses symbols and language familiar to a cross section of society (and not just to those actively involved in a faith community) enables the expression or acting out of feelings and their struggle to find understanding. The recent phenomenon of people, individually and collectively, expressing themselves through informal and formal ritual actions following the traumatic death of persons of significance is a mark of the importance ritual has in postmodern life. Gestures made in ritual moments provide a universal means of expressing grief and marking, with dignity, the importance of lives lost which meet, at least in part, some of the spiritual needs of those participating.

Bauman (1991) argues that to live in postmodern times is to live with an awareness of uncertainty. The certainty of modernity and its assurance that nature and all its ills could be overcome by scientific progress is no longer assumed. In a postmodern world where there is on one hand a growing realisation that the life of an individual, community, nation or, indeed, world is contingent; there is still the need for certainty, for security, deep within the psyche of human beings. The modern belief that knowledge could realise such certainty and with it security has not been achieved however much it is desired. Significant traumatic deaths and events which confront the assumed order of life and living and impinge on the life of local, national and global communities serve to underline the unpredictable nature of the postmodern world. For example, the shooting of youngsters in a Scottish, Russian or American school or university or the effects of bombings on the London underground.

Within such a context, there has been the rediscovery of the need for ritual: a communal acting out of the depth of loss and grief in the aftermath of such events. In ritual, communities, however transient, are formed. Therefore, not only is the need to do something when feeling helpless in the face of tragedy partially met so too is the deep need for human solidarity and contact at such a time. Bauman (1991, 246) refers to postmodernity as well as being an era of uncertainty, as 'also the age of community' typified by 'the lust for community, search for community, invention of community, imagining community'. Community (whether religious, cultural, political or a group of neighbours or like-minded people), postulates Bauman, provides shelter from the buffeting, fragmentation and tensions of postmodern life.

Ritual provides a culturally approved context which enables freedom from constraining cultural norms. Within the parameters of ritual, there is permission for the corporate expression of shared feelings, questions, wrestling and searching through the communal enactment of that which cannot be readily verbalised in a manner which transcends, yet allows room for, personal beliefs and worldviews in the face of trauma which challenges individual's preassumptive worlds. Rituals can potentially temporarily unify a disparate group who require a means by which to act out their inner response to a significant loss which challenges their worldview and belief system. For example, the spontaneous gathering of people on the streets of Madrid to light candles as they began to absorb the news of the death and maiming of many their fellow citizens due to the bombing of a commuter train. Furthermore, ritual as a response to death allows expression of lament for the loss of the certainty and sense of meaning which humanity craves.

The relatively recent ritual creation of roadside shrines of flowers and soft toys following traffic accidents or the leaving of other symbols of solidarity and expressions of grief (such as football stripes and scarves being draped at the scenes of the murders of young football supporters in Glasgow or at Hillsborough and Bradford football grounds following major disasters) are an embodied expression of that which is beyond speech in an increasingly socially acceptable way. Such acts not only enable those who are touched personally by such tragedy to 'do something' in the face of utter helplessness but also allow the wider community to express themselves when they are reminded of their own mortality and losses (actual and potential).

Likewise, mass gatherings, as people from all over the world flock to participate in ritual farewells to ionic figures of royal, religious and political significance, facilitate an outpouring of deeply held yet submerged feeling in a communal setting. Peter Preston (2005, 28) encapsulates beautifully the common motivation for such public acts when describing the scenes following Pope Jean Paul II's death:

There is no reason why ordinary citizens of our increasingly instant wired world shouldn't be allowed to weep alongside their leaders and peers, to bring their own circumstances to their traditional pomp.

New rituals too are being created to celebrate not just lament the death of those who have made an impact in the public domain. Following the death in November 2005 of Georgie Best, one of the greatest and most charismatic players to grace a football field, there was not just the well-worn ritual of media nostalgia but also a variation of the more familiar minute's silence before football matches. Up and down, Britain football fans, no matter what their creed, colour or local footballing allegiance, joined in a minute of celebration (clapping, cheering and chanting) to mark a life which lit up, enhanced and gave meaning to theirs. Such ritual involvement meets a profound need within humanity to collectively act out what is instinctively felt and deeply held.

Not all rituals are communal by design or intent. Some rituals, as well as death, have become privatised in postmodern society, especially with the advent of computer technology. It is now increasingly popular to memorialise a loved one on the worldwide web and visit that memorial as and when an individual or family wants. Pilgrimage to facilitate ritual remembering can now be done with our fingertips from anywhere in the globe not just in person at a graveside or park bench donated in memory of the deceased.

3

Grieving in a Postmodern World

End is in beginning;
And in beginning end:
Death is not loss, nor life winning;
But each and to each is friend.

Soutar (2005, 54)

Even in our birth there is ending, the cessation of our total dependence on our mothers for shelter and sustenance within the maternal womb; one ending on an ongoing journey of beginnings and endings, endings and new beginnings. Loss and bereavement, death and dealing with its impact are part of life from the very start. For many mothers soon after giving birth comes that dreaded thought that one day the baby they now hold will die. Moreover, Soutar's reflections on death and life being closely interrelated remind us that death is ultimately neither an adversary to be defeated nor a failure to be avoided at all costs. It is inherent part of human life. As Shuchter and Zisook (1993, 23) put it: 'Grief is a natural phenomenon that occurs after the loss of a loved one.'

However, grief in the past has been medicalised: 'a "condition" in need of diagnosis and treatment' (Joanna Briggs Institute 2006, 4). Similar modernist resonances can be found in contemporary Western society which reveal discomfort with overt grieving and the feelings associated with it. There is still a common desire for a person's grief to be overcome or worked through quickly so as not to remind the rest of the surrounding community of their mortality. 'The broken part heals even stronger than the rest', they say. But that takes awhile. And, 'Hurry up', the whole world says. They tap their feet. And it still hurts on rainy afternoons when the same absent sun gives no sign it will ever come back (Stafford 1993, 6 cited by Cole, Jr. [2005, 198]).

Frequently, after a few weeks or months in the workplaces and neighbourhoods that the bereaved inhabit, others expect them to have returned to their *premortem* condition. The deceased and the feelings of the bereaved individual are often no longer referred to or enquired after. However, not only are the bereaved irreversibly changed by the death of someone close but their grief is ongoing for a significant period as Stafford indicates. In fact, grief is not something the bereaved get over. It is something that is learnt to be lived with. The period of intensity and articulation thereof varies from person to person. Moreover, the circumstances of the death mourned also influences bereavement, for example, sudden or traumatic deaths have been shown to be more difficult to deal with (Parkes 1996). How any person expresses and lives with bereavement, how an individual or group mourns, will depend on the cultural and religious norms of the families and communities people belong to or have been brought up in.

> Death may happen in a moment but grief takes time; and that time is both an ordeal and a blessing. An ordeal in the sense that grief is often one of the most severe mental pains that we must suffer, and a blessing in the sense that we don't have to do it all at once. We can, to a degree, ration out our grief in bearable dosage; according to our circumstances we may choose to give full vent to grief and, like the Maoris, cry and shout and chant three days and nights on end; or we may stultify our grief, avoiding public show, and leak it, drip by drip, in secret, over many months. But sooner or later, in time, our grief will out, like truth, a harsh reminder of our own mortality. (Parkes 1984, *XI*)

Grief, the personal experience of the death of another, will touch us all during our lifetime. It is both an activity and something which has to be lived with and endured. Grief is a journey which involves both our inner and outer worlds; facets of our personhood which are private and public, conscious and otherwise. Painful though grief is 'resilience is the norm in the face of bereavement rather than the exception' (Dutton and Zisook 2005, 877).

What the bereaved may live through and experience as part of the painful and tortuous journey of grief paradoxically may offer new possibilities and potential growth when a loved one dies.

Dimensions of Grief

Shuchter and Zisook (1993, 43) offer a helpful generalised overview of the complexity of grief and the extent to which it can disturb the equilibrium of an individual's life and living.

> A prototypical life stress event, bereavement is associated with immense turmoil and stress . . . .Grief's duration may be prolonged, at times, even indefinite, and its intensity varies over time, from person to person, and culture to culture. It cannot be understood from a static or linear perspective; rather, a full appreciation of the grieving process requires attention to its diverse, multidimensional perspectives. These include affective and cognitive states, coping strategies, the continuing relationship with the deceased, changes in functioning, changes in relationships, and alterations in identity.

In order to outline such a multidimensional and all-embracing activity such as grief a framework is required to aid the description and explanation of its various facets.[1] Grief may be thought as having four dimensions:

---

1 This schema is developed from Peter Speck's (1997) reflections on the different levels at which a funeral is required to operate in order to meet the possible needs of the bereaved participating. Speck suggests three such dimensions—the psychological, theological or philosophical and sociological levels.

- A psychological level – the emotional and mental impact of bereavement. How such thoughts and feelings expressed are an integral part of the coping mechanisms developed by an individual, family or community to deal with grief.
- A spiritual level – the part of human make up that searches for meaning and purpose in death and bereavement. It is the part of humanity that tries to make sense of a situation of loss and find hope for the present and the future.
- A social level – in order to create and integrate rounded memories of the deceased into the fabric of their lives, there is a need for the bereaved to share and hear stories about their loved one in the company of others.
- A practical level – grieving involves carrying out practical tasks in relation to creating and organising rituals which mark the life and death of the deceased as well as performing tasks which their new role as a bereaved individual involves. For example, a widow may need to deal with the maintenance of her house and garden for the first time.

Each of these four levels or dimensions of grief is involved in an individual's, family's and community's response to the death of a significant person or persons, to a lesser or greater degree, and are all utilised as a means by which grief is dealt with. They will be returned to in order to discuss how a church representative aiding a family to create and participate in a relevant funeral may considerably help to meet their needs following the death of a loved one in a multiplicity of ways. These four aspects of grieving will now be explored more fully as well as how the internal world of the bereaved and their relationships with others are significantly impacted on by bereavement.

Psychological Dimension of Grief

Undoubtedly, the psychoanalytic approach of Sigmund Freud developed in the nineteenth century has informed much of the current understanding of the psyche's response to bereavement (Stroebe and Schut 2001). For Freud, grieving centred on a psychological response to the loss of an object (the focus in this case being a much loved individual) to which a person is deeply attached. Normally this involves, over a period, the withdrawal of emotional attachment from the deceased person and its investment into new objects or activities. In the case of pathological grief, or in Freudian terms melancholia (Freud 1957), the bereaved does not emotionally detach himself or herself from the deceased but the intense feelings are internalised. Thus, feelings of anger and the desire to blame the deceased for abandoning the bereaved are turned in on self which may lead in time to feelings of low self-esteem and self-loathing. Based on Freud's hypothesis, Walter (1996, 7) defines what grief as a psychological activity involves: 'the reconstitution of an autonomous individual who can in large measure leave the deceased behind and form new attachments. The *process* by which this is achieved is the working through and resolution of feelings'.

Though every individual deals with bereavement in their own particular manner, clinicians and researchers such as Lindemman (1944), Bowlby (1980) and Parkes (1972, 1986, 1996) have observed that there is a generalised pattern of psychological and behavioural response by the bereaved to the death of a loved one. Grief, according to Colin Murray Parkes (1996, 7) is a 'distinct psychological process' which involves a series of 'clinical pictures which blend into and replace one another'. Such an understanding of grief involves the bereaved passing through such phases, though not in a linear and ordered fashion, until he or she recovers. First, there is numbness or disbelief. Second, pining or heartfelt searching for the deceased associated with anger and protest against the loss. Third, this is followed by a period of disorganisation in which the bereaved attempts to readjust to the changes in his or her perceptions of how the world is ordered and understood now that the deceased is dead. Fourth, prior to living life more fully and lightly, though differently, once more the bereaved will experience a sense of despair or apathy and listlessness where life is more of a burden than a source of fulfilment. Parkes (1996) emphasises that such phases of grief are often revisited at different times in life set in motion by memories or occurrences associated with the deceased. Moreover, often the psychological impact of grief is not only articulated verbally but is also expressed psychosomatically.

To deal with the psychological adjustments to life and living following the death of a significant other, certain activities or work is required to be performed. William Worden (2002, 47) describes such a process as the tasks of mourning:

I To accept reality
II To experience the pain
III To adjust to the environment without loved one
    external adjustments
    internal adjustments
    spiritual adjustments
IV To relocate and memorialise loved one

The process Worden describes underlines how interwoven the different dimensions of grieving are. Adjusting to the external environment a bereaved person inhabits involves practical changes, for example, learning new skills and roles previously performed by a deceased spouse. Trying to deal with who they are *postmortem* as a person, involves the bereaved doing internal psychological work, as they may be bereft of their sense of self (at least in part) as well as a partner if previously they perceived, or even defined, themselves as a husband or wife or partner of the deceased. Spiritual adjustment will be outlined below, as will the social dimensions of grieving which help enable the relocation and memorialisation of a loved one.

Walter (1999, 106) refers to the 'clinical lore' that many berea-vement carers utilise in their work which has been absorbed from the influence of the early writings of Kubler-Ross (1969), Parkes (1972, 1984), Bowlby (1980) and Worden (1983). This is the received wisdom that the bereaved pass through a series of stages[2] or phases until they are able to let go of their intimate and intense feelings for the deceased and move on with life. Though their concepts of grief became more nuanced in their later work the fundamental ideas of these clinicians and researchers are still influential today. In the 1990s, Walter felt bereavement care was heavily reliant on a clinical lore which maintained it was essential for the bereaved to verbalise their feelings to deal appropriately with their grief, that grief was time limited and resolution of grief was required to enable normal life to be resumed. Moreover, if grief was not verbalised and was perceived to be prolonged by the surrounding community it was considered abnormal. Walter (1999, 157) feels that though clinical lore does accept everyone grieves differently 'it still makes authoritative claims about what is and is not healthy grieving'. Constructs and suggested frameworks of grief proposed by researchers and clinicians as descriptions have become for many carers, and thus the bereaved themselves, prescriptions as to how the bereaved should experience and deal with grief.

Spiritual Dimension

The spiritual dimension of our personhood is that aspect which seeks meaning and purpose in our experience of life and death, including importantly, bereavement (the spiritual aspect of our humanity is explored in more depth in the next chapter).

> Death makes philosophers of us all
> the prospect of it in reality
> disturbs time itself
> lifelong patterns fall from us

---

2   Elizabeth Kubler-Ross was an American psychiatrist whose work with the dying led to the development of a five-stage model for the anticipatory grief of the dying. This model was later applied to the grief of the bereaved. The bereaved in turn going through stage of denial, anger, bargaining, depression and acceptance.

as withered leaves lay bare the trees
in winter.

(Wallbank 1984, 12)

The finality of death and the significance of its impact not only make the majority of the bereaved philosophers but theologians also. The seeming passivity of God in the face of great suffering may be wrestled with, God's sense of justice and compassion doubted and the existence of a Greater Being called into question. Such lament has echoed in the voices of the bereft down through the centuries and is captured in the ancient words of the psalmist:

Rouse yourself, Lord; why do you sleep?
Awake! Do not reject us for ever.
Why do you hide your face,
heedless of our misery and our suffering?
For we sink down to the dust
and lie prone on the ground.
Arise and come to our aid;
for your love's sake deliver us.

(Psalm 44: 23–26)

Trying to make sense of death and find meaning in the possible pain endured by the deceased and by those bereaved themselves cause great spiritual distress. Existential questions when dealing with great loss are not only understandable but also commonplace and heartfelt.

Christopher Rush (2006, 94), a teacher and writer, encapsulates vividly such pain as he tries to make sense of the death of his wife from breast cancer:

Death seldom strikes one as a good idea at any time, but when a mother and wife is still young and strong and lovely, death arrives on the doorstep as a particularly brutal irrelevance, and there is some human longing to make it relevant, to make it mean something.

Social Dimension

In the 1990s, researchers[3] began to develop what previously had been a more peripheral theme in the reflections of those formulating models of grief;[4] that of the significance of bereaved persons integrating their dead loved one into their ongoing life story. Through the memory of the deceased being maintained by recollection and storytelling the bereaved over time may develop a transformed yet continuing relationship with that dead person which may inform, for example, decision-making at significant moments in the future life of the bereaved.

Grieving, thus, is a social as well as an individual process (Neimeyer 2005). In the telling and retelling of the story of the deceased and his or her relationship with them, and hearing from others their interpretation of the deceased's life, the bereaved may develop a more rounded biography of their loved one's life (Walter 1996). Moreover, perhaps with time, the bereaved may find some meaning and purpose in the deceased's life and make more sense of their death and the relationships they had, and continue to have, with those left behind. As when dealing with other life events and issues, when coping with grief 'human beings are meaning makers and weavers of narratives that give thematic significance to the plot structures of their lives' (Neimeyer 2005, 28).

The significance of reminiscing with others about a dead family member is not only for the purposes of meaning-making and maintaining 'continuing bonds' (Klass et al. 1996) with the deceased but it is also paradoxically to acknowledge their death. As Walter (1996, 19) puts it: 'Trying to grasp the reality of the deceased being gone but yet being here, and doing this through continually monitoring that reality by talking to those who knew her.' It is therefore, important for the bereaved to have

---

3   Such as Tony Walter (1996) in the United Kingdom and Dennis Klass, Phyllis Silvermann and Steven Nickmann (1996) in the United States.

4   For example, John Bowlby (1980) and Colin Murray Parkes (1986).

others around who are willing and able to participate in such storytelling and listening. Norman McCaig (1993, 411) captures beautifully the bittersweet nature of such social interaction as he remembers his dead wife as 'The salt of absence, the honey of memory.'

Therefore, if we are to take the social dimension of grieving seriously and an individual's need to maintain a real, though altered, relationship with their deceased loved one: 'The focus in facilitating mourning needs to be on how to change connections, to hold onto the relationship in a new perspective rather than on how to separate' (Silvermann and Klass 1996, 20). McCaig (2005) in his poem 'Praise of a Man' again offers insight into the nature of our ongoing connections with the deceased and his or her continued influence on our lives:

> He's gone: but you can see
> his tracks still, in the snow of the world.

Tom Gordon (2004), a Scottish hospice chaplain, emphasises the resonance between sociological and theological understandings of the importance to the bereaved of the maintenance of ongoing, but changed, relationships with their deceased loved ones. The social discourse of the bereaved with family and friends to develop and maintain memories of the deceased is similar to the theological discourse within Christian worship which talks of the communion of saints – the church in heaven having an ongoing connection with, and influence on, the church on earth.

However, maintaining a relationship with a dead loved one should not predominate life. As adjustments are made to life without the physical presence of the deceased and with time, there should be room for investment in other areas of life. Mitchell and Anderson (1983, 95) sum up healthy grieving:

> A lost loved one really does live on in memory, and that memory will colour our lives from that point onward, but

it need not and should not dominate our living. Proper grieving makes new attachments possible while living with old memories.

Practical Dimension

A key facet of grief is the bereaved having to deal with the practical tasks and activities which arise due to the death of someone close. For a widowed spouse or adult offspring, it may involve the unwanted task of arranging and paying for a funeral for the deceased. Other practical jobs to be done may include winding up a relative's estate; stopping the benefits they received and notifying various utility providers of their death. For a partner such tasks may involve taking on and learning new roles in life which hereto the deceased had performed in their relationship. Widows may have to learn how to balance finances, pay the bills and when to take the car to the garage. Widowers may have to learn how to cook, iron and how to use the washing machine. Such activities may provide a welcome distraction from dealing with the pain of grief or may accentuate feelings of sadness or anger that the person who formerly had performed these roles was no longer there. The learning and ownership of such new roles can be, with time, liberating and energising for some or burdensome and difficult for others.

Stroebe and Schut (1999) in their 'dual process model of coping with grief' give due attention to the practical dimension of grief and the significant role it can play in helping people to deal with it. They postulate that while living with the death of a loved one, bereaved persons oscillate from focussing on their feelings and ruminating on the death and its circumstances to being focussed on the practical tasks and new roles they have to carry out. Thus, Stroebe and Schut normalise behaviour which at times distracts the bereaved from their loss and its implications for their lives when they adopt a doing and adapting mode. The greater the length of time after the bereavement the more the bereaved will spend being 'restoration-orientated' than 'loss-orientated' though oscillation back to reminiscing and being sad may occur at any time in relation to certain events or thoughts.

Grief – Resolved or Accommodated?

Grief is not resolved after a certain time or after the performing of certain rituals. The rent, caused by bereavement, in the pattern of the life a bereaved person has woven for themselves *antemortem* is never repaired. It becomes part of the bereaved's new *postmortem* fabric of life. Wienrich and Speyer (2003, 327) describe it in terms of physical injury:

> Grief is a natural healing reaction to loss. It is not unlike trying to heal a wound after an injury occurs. A minor wound may heal quickly – a major one is another matter; healing may take place over time, but the scars will always be there.

Such wounds are partially reopened or the residual scars at least become inflamed or more apparent at certain times of the year or living through certain trigger experiences.

> These days she cries
> her short fierce greit
> only on anniversaries.
> I hold her till its done.
> (Grieg 2001, 44)

Grief, as the Liverpudilian poet Roger McGough (2006, 169) suggests, is not timebound:

> We fall to the earth like leaves
> Lives as brief as footprints in snow
> No words express the grief we feel
> I feel I cannot let her go.
>
> For she is everywhere.

Walking on the windswept beach Talking in
the sunlit square.
Next to me in the car
I see her sitting there.

At night she dreams me
and in the morning the sun does not rise.
My life is as thin as the wind
And I am done with counting stars.

She is gone, she is gone.
I am her sad music, and I play on, and on,
and on.

Accommodation of the experience of grief into the life of
the bereaved is, thus, a more suitable way of thinking about
how people deal with grief in the long term rather than recov-
ery, resolution or closure (Klass et al. 1996).

The Problems of Grieving in a Postmodern Era

At the beginning of the twenty-first century in the majority of
the Western world the bereaved are free to grieve as they wish,
as long as they don't grieve too intensely for too long. If they
do, the danger is that they become ostracised and ignored as
their family, colleagues and neighbours tire of hearing the same
stories recounted or become embarrassed by high expressed
emotion at work or in the street. Postmodern culture encour-
ages us to be autonomous beings; to follow our own path to
our own chosen destination and is an era in which death itself
has been privatised and medicalised. Grieving in contemporary
society is a journey into the unknown; into a desert where
there are no cairns or signposts to guide the disorientated
traveller, especially a first-time one. At a time of considerable
bewilderment and confusion there are few, if any, cultural
norms which provide benchmarks for the bereaved as to what
are normal feelings to have or how to articulate or enact those

feelings. As Walter (1999, 208) points out: 'It is all very well to say that everyone grieves differently, but people need to have some idea of what to expect when they, or others, are grieving.' This leads Walter to conclude that in our present-day society grief is 'under-regulated'; there is a lack of means by which grief is normalised and the distress the bereaved are feeling may be accentuated by wondering whether their feelings and how they deal with them are normal or not.

Some would consider this liberating in our postmodern era in which there are deemed to be no overarching narratives informing an individual's behaviour and worldview. However, as Walter (1999) points out, there is a need for people in their vulnerability and anxiety to know that their feelings are normal and appropriate and, thus, a need for some external points of reference with which to gauge their own experience and feelings. He suggests that the regulation of grief may currently be done by a value system or framework which is now outdated for many people (since at a time of grief no one is in a fit state to change the rulebook); a funeral shaped by Christian tradition and liturgy. Therefore, for many non-religious people a traditional, prescribed religious funeral may add to, instead of lessening, their feelings of disorientation and lack of control.

Bereavement Care in a Postmodern Era

If bereavement care is to meet the real needs of the bereaved, carers have to begin where people are rather than where we assume where they might be. Attention requires to be given to the four dimensions of grieving outlined above, or at least the bereaved should be given the opportunity to have their needs responded to in these various aspects of their grieving. The bereaved should be given the time, space and permission to verbalise their feelings and tell the story of their loved one should they need to do so. The opportunity to search for meaning and attempt to make sense of suffering and God's lack of response to it should be offered but not imposed. People should not be made to feel guilty when they go into practical mode to cope and try to escape, consciously or unconsciously, the searing pain of loss for a while. After all as T. S. Eliot (cited by Gordon 2006, 55) reminds us, 'Human kind cannot bear very much reality.' Indeed, ritual leaders from the church (along with representatives of other caring groups, such as hospital staff or the funeral director) are required to encourage some practical activity as there is a need to share information with the bereaved about practical issues surrounding disposal and ritual so that they can make informed choices.

In the past 20 years, with the development of an increasing variety of ways of understanding the experience of grief based on an array of qualitative and quantitative research projects with a range of bereaved populations, grief is no longer simply thought of as a linear process which moves from psychological disturbance to equilibrium (Neimeyer 2005). This has implications for the bereavement carer and ritual leader to provide appropriate bereavement support, including helping to co-create and share in relevant funerals the carer must have up to date knowledge of the different dimensions and theories of grieving rather than simply relying on the 'clinical lore' of the stage or phase models so prevalent in practice in the latter part of the twentieth century.

4

Spiritual Care of the Bereaved

Traditionally within Western society the Church has offered solace and support to the bereaved not just in the form of ritual marking of the life and death of the deceased but also through individual and communal care and attention. Even in our postmodern context many who otherwise are not in contact with a local faith community seek out the services of church representatives, working in congregational, parish or secular institutional settings, for assistance with funerals. Before going on to explore what this may involve, the broader context of care, within which the process of the ritualisation of death and mourning may be facilitated by a church representative, will be outlined.

Since biblical times, care has been offered to those in the spiritual and emotional turmoil of grief by individuals and groups representing faith communities as well as collectively by the whole community itself. For example, Paul's first pastoral letter to the new church at Thessalonica contains support and encouragement for a community who were grieving which was relevant to their context, beliefs and feelings (1 Thessalonians 4: 13). As has already been explored the predominant metanarrative influencing the value systems and worldviews of those living in the West has been Judeo-Christian until the latter part of the twentieth century. Until recent decades, those not closely affiliated with a local church would still be reasonably familiar with the language, symbols, stories and metaphors central to Christian life and worship. This offered a shared framework within which the significant issues and moral dilemmas experienced when dealing with major life events could be reflected upon or interpreted. In our postChristian

era fewer individuals and families utilise such resources to articulate and explore struggles in relation to their beliefs, experiences, hopes and fears about life, death and what may be
beyond. This chapter will outline the essence of how church
representatives may care for the bereaved in a manner appropriate to their needs, perceptions and feelings. The different
forms such spiritual care takes, depending on the particular
worldview of the bereaved seeking support, will be outlined.
Moreover, the relationship between these different aspects of
care for the spiritual dimension of the bereaved's humanity will
be explored. It will be argued that bereavement care shared
within the Christian community, where the Christian metanarrative is the main resource utilised to aid reflection on, and
reinterpretation of, the deceased's story and the survivor's grief
is pastoral care. In such a pastoral relationship there may be
times when the encounter or encounters become more like
spiritual direction where the main focus of the interaction is
the bereaved's feelings about, and relationship with, God rather
than the bereaved individual trying to make sense of their situation of loss in light of the God story. What is offered, as church
representatives working in both local community and institutional settings help create and perform funerals with those for
whom the Christian metanarrative is alien, will be termed person-centred spiritual care. In such situations the ritual leader
seeks to encourage the bereaved to utilise appropriate narratives or resources which are familiar and/or are helpful to them
as they seek to comprehend their loss and put it in some sort of
context.

Spirituality

The spiritual aspect of every individual contributes much to
what makes each and everyone of us unique as human beings.
It is intimately intertwined with the other core elements of our
humanity – our physicality and sexuality,[1] as well as the social

and psychological aspects of our being. When one of these key features is touched to any degree of depth by experience then the others are affected also. For example, in the immediacy of the death of a loved one a bereaved individual may feel considerable anxiety and fear, physically experienced as tightness in the chest. Such a subjective experience of abandonment may cause them to need the reassuring presence and touch of a close friend or family member. This may momentarily replace, or alternatively paradoxically be a reminder of, the loss of the physical intimacy provided hitherto by a deceased partner. Such feelings of separation and desolation may also be associated with profound existential questions.

The spiritual dimension of our personhood significantly shapes and influences our individuality and how we relate to others and the world around us, as well as how we make sense of our life and our living. This spiritual element in all of us seeks possibilities to transcend any present trying circumstances, to hope and to dream. Our spirit also desires opportunity for our self to relax, to be and to allow our senses to playfully and creatively roam. At a deep level we seek to love and be loved, to be connected to others, yet maintain our own beliefs, values and sense of identity (adapted from Bartel 2004). Yet what this essential component of our humanity actually is eludes precise definition and to seek to succinctly describe its essence is to detract from its fluidity and inherent dynamism. Mystery and otherness are part of what spirituality is.

---

1   Sexuality is not merely the genital expression of our feelings. It is also relates to how any of us feels about living in our bodies and relating to others as physical bodies.

Sexuality is our self-understanding and way of being in the world as male and female. It includes our appropriation of our attitudes and characteristics which have been culturally defined as male and female. It involves our affectional orientation towards others of the opposite and/or same sex. It includes our attitudes towards our own bodies and those of others. (Nelson 1979, 17–8)

In the past, the term spiritual was closely associated with the realm of religious institutions and practices, and indeed was often equated with formalised religion, corporate worship and private prayer. The spiritual journey in a Christian context was, and still is, thought of as a person's ongoing relationship with God. Canadian pastoral theologian Jean Stairs (2000, 10) says this: 'Our *spirituality* is simply the way we express our belief in and experience God in the world.' For some Christians, their awareness of their spirituality, where God is to be discerned on their inward and outward journey through life, is deepened by entering into a relationship of spiritual direction.

However, use of the term spirituality has broadened in the postmodern era and is now no longer just confined to utilisation within communities of faith, Christian or otherwise, where believers seek a deeper understanding of God's relationship with themselves, the church and the wider world.

> 'Spirituality' now refers to our relationship with the sacredness of life, nature, and the universe. . . . As times move on, we find we are able to define spirituality less and less, because it includes more and more, becoming a veritable baggy monster containing a multitude of activities and expectations.

> Spirituality has become diverse, plural, manifold, and seems to have countless forms of expression, many of which are highly individualistic and personal. Spirituality is now for everyone, and almost everyone seems to be involved, but in radically different ways. It is an inclusive term, covering all pathways that lead to meaning and purpose. It is concerned with connectedness and related-ness to other realities and existences, including other people, society, the world, the stars, the universe and the holy. It is typically intensely inward, and most often involves an exploration of the so-called inner or true self, in which divinity is felt to reside. (Tacey 2004, 38)

The core of the concept of spirituality in the twenty-first century is becoming more of who each of us really is.

> This ability of persons to self-determine his or her life, is perhaps the most fundamental example of the spiritual nature of the person. . . . This is the one chance we have to be the particular person we know we can be. (Morgan 1993, 8 [cited by Bregman 2004, 165])

No longer are we confined to utilising the resources of any one particular religious or cultural grouping in our quest for self-realisation and meaning-making. As a society we have far greater access to the insights, ritual practices and approaches to worship of a myriad of religions, reflective communities and spiritual advisors from which we can select as aids to growth those which suit our individual needs best. However, it is important to note that though the term spirituality in our post-modern world encompasses a far greater range of practices and is more person-centred than God-centred, it still includes in its overarching umbrella the Christian understanding of developing a deeper relationship with God. Bregman (2004, 165) puts it another way: 'Religion . . . organizes and provides a cultural framing for this underlying core of "spirituality." Religion is not universal, nor is it necessary to our humanity; spirituality is both.'

Tacey (2004, 39), however, is more guarded about the opportunities that spirituality affords people in their search for meaning and purpose in life. 'Although willed into existence by a collective aspiration, new spirituality is not collective, but is a personal experience. This is both its triumph and, of course, its severe limitation.'

In the ebb and flow of daily life and weekly routine people may or may not take time to contemplate who they are, what is important to them and how they interpret their life's experience or reflect on how they live through influences their beliefs and way of understanding the world and their place in it. Fewer people are certainly doing so within the context of faith communities and a diet of regular corporate worship. Men and women are, however, reflecting in such a way when their health and well-being is threatened. For example, when confronted with having to face up to living with chronic disease and/or disability, their own mortality or the death of someone they love. Therefore, it is not surprising that it has been from a variety of healthcare professions (particularly nursing, medicine and chaplaincy) that a plethora of research and writing has arisen in the past 20 years in the Western world in the field of spirituality. Such work has greatly influenced contemporary understandings of the spiritual aspect of our humanity as being a universal attribute.

Spiritual Need

In times of trauma, transition and adjustment the bereaved have a myriad of thoughts, feelings, questions and doubts within them, many of which are difficult to articulate. Each person living with loss will have a unique experience and way of living with bereavement but all will have spiritual needs. As a working definition of spiritual need within the context of bereavement care the following may be used:

> Spiritual need is that aspect of an individual's personhood which seeks to make sense of, and find meaning in, the present moment. Any such exploration is done in light of an individual's previous life experience and aspirations for the future and involves, potentially, consideration of any significant element of their unique life story. (Kelly 2007, 83)

Swede Levov, the central character in Philip Roth's Pulitzer Prize winning novel *American Pastoral* seems to have the perfect life – wealth, health, family, friends, athletic prowess and fulfilment. Set in the backdrop of the Vietnam War, Levov's idyll is shattered when his idealistic, though troubled, daughter blows up a local store as an anti-war gesture and in doing so murders three innocent people. His distress is great – grieving for the innocent daughter he once knew, the ordered life he once lived and the civil and domestic stability he expected for himself, for his family and his country. Swede's whole worldview is in tatters and such a significant bereavement impacts profoundly on his whole being. Roth (1998, 81) describes his character's spiritual distress in the following way:

> He had learnt the worst lesson that life can teach – that it makes no sense. And when that happens happiness is never spontaneous again. It is artificial and, even then, bought at the price of an obstinate estrangement from oneself and one's history. The nice gentle man with his mild way of dealing with conflict and contradiction, the confident ex-athlete sensible and resourceful in any strug-gle had come up against the adversary who is not fair – the evil ineradicable from human dealings – and he is finished. He whose natural nobility was to be exactly what he seemed to be has taken in far too much suffering to be naively whole again. Never again, will the Swede be con-tent in trusting the old Swedian way that, for the sake of his second wife and their three boys – for the sake of *their* naïve wholeness – he ruthlessly goes on pretending to be.

Swede's great spiritual need is to find meaning in his layers of loss within his own specific religious, cultural and familial context. His premorbid personality and the specific circum-stances he found himself in also influenced the way he sought to meet his needs – to seek to understand his daughter, himself and his family's relationships at a deeper level. However, the scars remain; his way of being and dealing with life is perma-nently altered though superficially he acts out the life he perceives others need him to. How often is this not the way the bereaved may deal with distress because of familial or societal convention and pressures?

It is important to emphasis that spiritual need is not to be equated with religious need, to do so is to limit the former. For a person who is actively seeking to live out their Christian faith, doing so by participating in religious activities may meet their religious needs and some but not all of their spiritual needs. For example, in performing some of the religious duties I am involved in as a hospital chaplain (sharing prayers or communion at a bedside or in the chapel), worshipping on a Sunday as part of a local church community and desiring to take time each day to reflect, pray and read the Bible does give purpose in my life and offers me a framework of values and beliefs to utilise when engaging with moral dilemmas and life experiences which throw up existential and theological questions. Furthermore, in my reflecting I seek to glimpse something of God in my encounters with others, in nature and in the political and social contexts and struggles I am involved in and am aware of. This I do with the aid of regular spiritual direction. However, such activities and times of stillness only partly meet my spiritual needs. I also find meaning and enjoyment from playing rugby and socialising with my teammates, hill walking, reading, listening to music and most of all from being with the people I love. These latter pursuits are not religious but for me and countless others they are potentially deeply spiritual and through them and in them I find a purpose in living and on occasions find a touching point with the transcendent. Finding meaning in life in such ways is part of what it means to be human and when essential components of our individual and collective ways of normally meeting our spiritual needs are taken from us or inhibited in some way spiritual distress is experienced.

Spiritual Care

The individual and collective response to spiritual distress, such as Swede Levov's, is termed spiritual care. Significantly, for the purposes of this discussion in specific relation to bereavement care and the construction of funerals the term spiritual care will envelop two different nuances. First, spiritual care as the overarching and inclusive term used to describe a helping relationship formed between persons, no matter what their beliefs and worldviews, to attend to the needs of that universal dimension of our human makeup which is termed spiritual. Such spiritual care includes that which has traditionally been known as pastoral care and spiritual direction, yet offers creative transforming possibilities to a broader range of bereaved individuals, families and communities. Careful assessment of the individual's or family's spiritual needs involves listening, observing and an active checking out with the bereaved of what their feelings, perceptions and beliefs actually are is required to provide sensitive care. Discernment on the part of the carer is also required to gently encourage the bereaved to refer to resources and narratives relevant to them to aid their processing and reinterpretation of their experience.

What spiritual care is in essence no matter what approach is taken to meet the needs of the bereaved by the church representative will be explored after looking at what these methods are and when they might be utilised.

Figure 4.1 below visually outlines what spiritual care as a broad term used within the context of care of the bereaved may be and the types of care encompassed within it. This figure will be referred to later in the discussion of how its various components interrelate.

This brings us on to the second and more limited meaning of the term spiritual care used within this book.

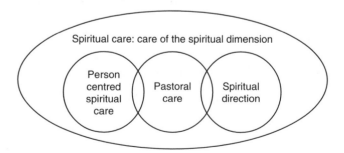

Figure 4.1 Spiritual Care: the Variety of Approaches Involved.

Person-centred Spiritual Care

All good bereavement care provided by church representatives begins where the bereaved are on their journey of grief and respects their worldview, values and understanding of their experience. Where a ritual leader seeks to co-construct a funeral with a family whose frame of reference for dealing with the mysteries of life, death and life after death does not include the Christian metanarrative, the spiritual care offered is termed person centred. It is person centred in that God has no relevance for the bereaved and to seek to proactively insist they reflect on their experience of grief and relationship with the deceased in light of the Christ story is inappropriate.[2] Such spiritual care seeks to help the bereaved to make sense of their experience with reference to their own particular worldview in one to one relationships or in shared ritual moments and does not seek to impose beliefs and narratives which are alien and, thus, irrelevant.

Pastoral Care

Pastoral care is a particular form of spiritual care offered by church representatives and communities relating to those whose lives also are informed by the Christ story. It is also not just about offering bereaved individuals' time and space in which to seek meaning and purpose in their experience of loss. Pastoral care may also be given and received within corporate worship or through ritual enactment. What a community of faith in which pastoral care is given and received 'can offer is a storied context of ultimate meaning within which life can be lived (and interpreted)'[3] (Gerkin 1997, 103). Within such a community a shared language and narrative is available to utilise when engaging with questions of meaning and suffering.

---

2   It may be that the deceased had Christian beliefs but not the bereaved or vice versa. An exploration of dealing with the complexities of such a situation and how respective needs or wishes may be met or respected can be found in the next chapter.

3   The words in parentheses here are mine.

[O]ne of the fundamental structures of care that life in a community of faith can and should offer is a story or a grammar – a way of speaking about people's circumstances – that can connect people's life experience with the ultimate context of meaning contained in the Christian gospel. (Gerkin 1997, 103)

In the context of such communal activity 'The task of pastoral practitioners is to connect the divine and human narratives so deeply that the stories we tell and rituals we enact will diminish fragmentation and bind together believing communities' (Anderson and Foley 1998–99, 22). Enabling individuals to feel that they are not living or dealing with loss in isolation but are participants in wider social networks and that they belong within, and are significant to, worshipping communities of faith is central to the act of pastoral care (Brueggemann 1991). Therefore, whether offered in an office or a front room, in church or in a crematorium, pastoral care 'presupposes that it is care that is given and received within the matrix of relationships which constitute a community of faith, in this case the Christian Church' (Lyall 2001, 63).

Following the death of an individual or members of a family or local faith community where meaningful funerals are sought to be constructed with the bereaved, representatives of the church may develop existing connections with the bereaved or have to form new ones to offer sensitive pastoral care. In such a context offering pastoral care is:

to enter into a helping relationship motivated by love and compassion in which an individual or persons in relationship may deepen their understanding of self and their experience, of each other and/or God within their particular network of relationships in light of, and where appropriate utilising the resources of, the Christ story.

This may involve helping the bereaved to locate the place of the deceased in God's story (Lynch and Willows 2000) as well as the bereaved's personal story and the narrative of the local church and surrounding community. Moreover, sensitive pastoral care may enable the bereaved persons' loss and wrestling with questions of theodicy and suffering to be perceived anew within the wider human and divine story. It may be within the context of the ritualisation of the deceased's life and death that such insights may be glimpsed and reflected on over time. Such pastoral care permitting the sharing and enactment of personal, familial, communal and divine stories potentially offers those involved a greater narrative within which to reframe individual stories of loss – a narrative which offers the opportunity for transformation and hope (Anderson and Foley 1998).

Spiritual Direction

Spiritual direction is another aspect of spiritual care which occurs within the realms of a community of faith. It takes place within a contractual, ongoing relationship between a church representative trained in spiritual accompaniment and the church member requesting direction.

> Spiritual direction is concerned with nourishment of the life of prayer, the inner life. It seeks to help a person interpret the movements of the Spirit, and to distinguish the voice of God from other voices within the person. (Leech 1987, 265)

Spiritual directors, those sought out by Christians seeking to listen to God's voice more attentively in the midst of their experience of life and living in relationship with others, are individuals with the gift of discernment whose spiritual accompaniment of others is informed by their own experience of life and prayer. Moreover, they will have training in theological reflection and possess an openness to the transcendent (Leech 1977). Thomas Merton (cited by Leech 1977, 89), a Carmelite monk and prolific writer on the spiritual life says this: 'A spiritual director is then one who helps another to recognize and follow the inspirations of grace in his life, in order to arrive at the end to which God is leading him.'

It may be that a person already engaged in spiritual direction may become bereaved or indeed bereavement may be the stimulus for seeking accompaniment. Further, within a pastoral relationship following the death of a significant other a discerning church representative may offer some spiritual direction, not as an ongoing formal 'shared spiritual journey' (Stairs 2000, 189) but as a more immediate response to a time of vulnerability and distress when, for example, a bereaved person voices their concerns about their current inability to pray and or how distant they feel from God.

The Relationship between Spiritual Care, Pastoral Care and Spiritual Direction

In his insightful article 'Pastoral Counseling or Spiritual Direction: What's the Difference?' Tom Hart (2005), a psychotherapist and spiritual director, describes a spectrum of helping professionals (see Figure 4.2) with appropriate gifts and training who may offer on a one to one basis help to others within the context of a relationship in which they are listened to and affirmed. On the far left of his continuum are the psychotherapists for whom religious belief has no personal meaning. They are interested, within the therapeutic relationships they form, in past experiences, behaviour patterns and feelings not on the potential transformative role of the Christian metanarrative. On the far right of the spectrum are the spiritual directors who seek to develop a person's discernment of God's voice in their life and who utilise in their approach the stories and methods of prayer and reflection of their tradition. Those seeking the help of pastoral counsellors and pastoral carers (found in the middle of Hart's spectrum of carers) are concerned with personal growth or tackling a particular problem and want to do so not through in-depth analysis of their psyche or advice

Figure 4.2   Helping Professionals Providing a Spectrum of Services (adapted from Hart 2005, 8).

on prayer but by talking through their situation and reinterpreting it in light of the Christian story.

In his discussion of this model Hart describes how rarely these helpers are 'pure types' offering care which is clearly defined. For example, a church member may choose to enter into a pastoral relationship with their minister to talk about how he is struggling with his grief following the death of his partner. However, as the relationship develops it may at some point become more like spiritual direction as the survivor seeks advice as to how to live with his anger at, and inability to pray to, a God who has let his loved one suffer profoundly before death. In relation to the consideration of church representatives working to create and share meaningful funerals with the bereaved, who may or may not be familiar with, or influenced by, the Christian metanarrative it may be helpful to adapt Hart's concept of helping professionals providing a spectrum of services to explore the continuum of approaches to providing spiritual care provided by ritual leaders depending on their skills and ability and the needs of the bereaved.

Any helping relationship offered by a church representative which seeks to give an individual or a group of persons time and space in which to try to verbalise, explore or simply acknowledge and be with their distress may be termed spiritual care. If such care is done within a shared framework of Christian faith, utilising where appropriate the language, metaphors, stories and rituals of that faith to reinterpret their experience, then the care offered is pastoral. Owing to a limited number of the bereaved in our postmodern world belonging to the church or who are at least familiar with the resources that the Christian community utilises to engage with the mysteries of life and death, only a proportion of spiritual care is pastoral in nature. Likewise, only a small part of the support offered by church representatives to bereaved persons will consist of spiritual direction. However, to make clear distinctions between person-centred spiritual and pastoral care, and pastoral care and spiritual direction is to be oversimplistic.

In the provision of pastoral care there is a dialogue between an individual's particular story and the story of the Christian community to which they belong. Such a relationship 'always involves placing the caring minister somewhere between loyalty to and representation of the Christian story, on one hand, and empathic attention to the particularity of life stories on the other' Gerkin (1997, 112). For the American pastoral theologian Charles Gerkin, pastoral care involves the carer being in a place of tension as she helps another to make real connections between their story as they perceive it and the Christian story.

In model being considered here, in relation to care of the spiritual dimension by church representatives, in some situations (depending on the bereaved persons' worldview) more attention is paid to a person's unique perceptions, beliefs and feelings and in others the church representative's focus is on helping the bereaved not only to recall and reflect upon their story in light of the overarching metanarrative that influences carer and bereaved alike but also, on occasions, how to be more open to the One who is involved in both particular and grand narratives. Thus, in some instances pastoral care offered may almost merge, and certainly overlap (see figure 4.1), with person-centred spiritual care and in others be indistinguishable from spiritual direction. The role of a church representative in seeking to co-construct and share relevant funerals with families is therefore fluid. Not only will she have to utilise different approaches to providing spiritual care when supporting different people, she may also have to move from one approach to another during a single encounter. Therefore, ritual leaders seeking to meet the spiritual needs of a bereaved family through

Spiritual care: care of the spiritual dimension

Person-centred————————Pastoral Care————————Spiritual Direction
Spiritual Care
(emphasis on   (emphasis on God)
bereaved's story)

Figure 4.3   Providing Spiritual Care: a Spectrum of Approaches.

helping to co-construct and share with them in meaningful funerals have to work within, and along, a spectrum of approaches to providing spiritual care (see Figure 4.3). Much will depend on what informs the personal and collective stories of family members and their ability to articulate their needs and perspectives in the confusion of their acute grief as well as the discernment and training of the spiritual carer. Definitions of different aspects of care for the human spirit are, thus, far from precise. The boundaries between them are unclear and their meanings evolve with time and context, as has been shown in relation to the use of term spiritual. Such fluidity also applies to pastoral care. As Lyall (2001) points out pastoral care has many dimensions and nuances[4] and is a term which has become utilised outside communities of faith in recent years. For example, supportive care offered within schools, colleges and universities to pupils and students by members of staff is often termed 'pastoral' where neither carer or cared for may be significantly influenced by the Christian metanarrative.

Further complicating any effort to succinctly define aspects of spiritual care is that during the process of co-constructing funerals it is not infrequent that a bereaved family may have little knowledge of the Christian metanarrative but they may well wish the ritual leader to call upon a greater being for help for them in their time of grief or ask that the ritual leader commit their deceased loved one into the love and care of God during his funeral. Though the majority of the care offered

---

4   The important political dimension of pastoral care, for example, is out with the consideration of this book.

within such a relationship with a bereaved family is person-centred spiritual care in nature, it may be that it comes close to being pastoral in nature. However, for such a family the Christian metanarrative is not their overriding reference point in trying to interpret and make sense of their experience and nor is it the primary resource they draw from to articulate their inner world. The bereaved in our postmodern society utilise language, metaphors and ritual acts from the cultural milieu which they inhabit to inform their response to death, including their interaction with the media, their family and community culture and a wide range of resources and traditions, both religious and secular. The Christian tradition is, therefore, seen as one potential resource amongst many that may contain a sentiment, a specific belief, image, action, poem or phrase which helps the bereaved articulate their grief and reaction to it and thus, help to meet some of their spiritual. In an era devoid of common metaphors, images and a shared language to express the mysteries of life, death and significant issues of belief around both, the bereaved do often choose religious resources to help express themselves, whether by default or preference, when given a range of options to do so in the construction of a funeral with a church representative (this issue is explored more fully in the next chapter). Therefore, although bereaved persons may not choose or give any indication that they wish to utilise the Christian story as a means to reinterpret their family story and experience of grief, they may well wish to draw from the rich seam of resources from the Christian tradition to give expression to their feelings, experience and aspirations.[5]

The Essence of Spiritual Care of the Bereaved

There is a comfort in the strength of love;
'Twill make a thing endurable, which else

---

5   This is more fully explored in Chapter 5.

Would overset the brain, or break the heart.
(From 'A Pastoral Poem', Wordsworth, 1990
cited by Carroll 2001, 90)

Spiritual care of the bereaved offered by a representative of the church, in whatever form, is primarily about the embodiment of Christ's love. However, it is more than about offering *agape*; it is also about being open enough to receive it. Spiritual care is fundamentally about being with another rather than telling them what to do or believe in or, indeed, doing something for or to them (Campbell 1986).

The essence of what spiritual care is when embodied by a member of the Christian faith community is encapsulated by Lyall (2001, 96): 'One implication of the incarnation is that the communication of Christian truth is relational and not propositional.' Words and actions may be of importance but they are secondary to, and evolve from, the quality and depth of relationship established. Hart (2005, 11), a psychotherapist and spiritual director, reiterates this by pointing to the carer's ability to form and maintain a helping relationship in which the client or directee can be himself and grow and learn within such a context as being the basis of a potentially therapeutic relationship. He describes how clients or directees refer to such relationships: 'I feel safe with you. I know you care for me. I can talk freely about anything. You listen respectfully and carefully. You are wise and gentle, yet honest with me. I know you believe in me, and have hope for me.'

Meeting a bereaved individual's or family's spiritual needs involves beginning where they are on their particular journey of grief not where we assume they are, where we want them to be or how we want them to be behaving. Therefore, person-centred spiritual care, pastoral care or spiritual direction involving the bereaved requires respect for the other's story, experience, beliefs and worldview as well their way of dealing with their loss:

don't tell me that I mourn too much
and I won't tell you that you mourn too
much ...
don't tell me that I mourn in the wrong way
and I won't tell you that you mourn in the
wrong way

I may get it wrong, I will get it wrong, I have
got it wrong
but don't tell me.

(Rosen 2004, 94)

Spiritual care of the bereaved importantly begins with the offering of the presence of self alongside another at a time of distress. In doing so a carer may utilise learnt skills of active listening and insights gained from different psychotherapeutic approaches but at its very core is the carer's ability to make himself or herself available to the other in the present moment. Pembroke (2002, 4–5) emphasises this key facet of spiritual care giving

> in the absence of giving of self, of real emotional availability, of genuine love and fidelity, they (skills and techniques) will only be minimally effective in facilitating healing and growth. Put differently, a person feels genuinely cared for not so much because she has received expert psychological assistance, important though that is, but rather because she has received the gift of self from her pastor or counsellor.

The cartoonist Bill Watterson illustrates much of what has been described above as the essence of spiritual care in one of his cartoon strips illustrating the adventures and life experiences of Calvin, a six-year-old American boy, and his best friend Hobbes, a stuffed tiger who comes to life in his imagination. On reflecting in bed at night with Hobbes on the events of that day, Calvin ruminates over having found a baby racoon which has been run over and then subsequently dies. In the first two of four illustrations, Watterston depicts Calvin wrestling with the mystery of death and the injustice of those who die before life has been fully experienced. In the third picture Calvin vents his anger and frustration in the form of more existential questions to his friend, who remains silent yet clearly attentive to what is being expressed both verbally and non-verbally. In the final illustration the two friends are now to be found under Calvin's bed both looking perplexed and wrung out by Calvin's attempts to find meaning and purpose in the life and death of the racoon and his engagement with mortality. It is only then for the first time that Hobbes speaks and even then, it is a question: 'Why is it always night when we talk about such things?' In this short series of sketches Hobbes embodies sensitive spiritual care of those who are bereft. He accepts his friend as he is and by his availability and non-judgemental attitude gives Calvin permission to be as he needs to be at that moment in time and to articulate how he feels in his own way. In doing so Hobbes normalises Calvin's experience and expression of his grief. He does not offer his friend any absolutes or answers to his questions, religious or otherwise, but instead by his attentive presence Hobbes affirms Calvin at a time of vulnerability and confusion as well as validating Calvin's own search for understanding.

Hobbes' relationship with Calvin in his distress and searching epitomises the relationship church representatives should seek to have with the bereaved in the immediacy of the death of a loved one as they seek to co-construct a meaningful funeral for the departed and those who grieve for them. It is only out of a relationship where the spiritual carer is attentive to, and affirming of, the story of the deceased as told by the bereaved as well as the experience of the bereaved and their particular expression of their grief that authentic ritual action and story telling can evolve. Only in the context of such a relationship of trust can the spiritual needs of the bereaved be assessed in any depth and a meaningful ritual response begin to be co-authored by both carer and the bereaved (where sought). In short, sensitive spiritual care begins with an attentive presence and the building up of a rapport with the bereaved, encouraging an individual's or family's story to be told and heard, their needs assessed and then, and only then, any appropriate verbal or enacted response made or suggested. Such a response may include referral to a colleague or another more appropriate agency, for example a Humanist celebrant or an organisation offering ongoing bereavement support such as Cruse.

Crucially, spiritual care of the bereaved as well as involving being with and actively doing (listening, sharing information and options as well as possible referral) also involves leaving. This will be further explored in the next chapter as we look at the process of co-constructing funerals but leaving bereaved relatives on their own (either as a group or as individuals), giving them time to themselves is an important part of care of the bereaved between the death of their loved one and the funeral. Time alone is required for the bereaved to begin to process their thoughts and feelings and to mull over decisions that have to be made regarding disposal, ritual marking and other practical and legal tasks that have to be performed (though some of these decisions may already have been made prior to death). Sometimes the best spiritual care we can offer is to leave and let a person grieve in their own way in their own time. Discerning when to stay and when to go is never easy as the cues we pick up may be mixed but checking out with the bereaved what they actually need at that moment in time is always helpful; and it may well be time and space on their own. Edward Thomas (1987) in his poem 'Lights Out' (cited by Carroll 2001, 93) reflects on the harsh reality of being alone when dying. The sentiments in this poem are also applicable to the bereaved on their journey into the unknown; though both the dying and bereaved may be accompanied, dying and learning to live with bereavement is something all of us ultimately have to do on our own.

There is not any book
Or face of dearest look
That I would not turn from now
To go into the unknown
I must enter, and leave, alone,
I know not how.

Letting go of the bereaved and their pain, actually and metaphorically, is also vital for the well-being of any church representative providing spiritual or pastoral care before moving on to care for the next person or deal with another situation of loss. Ultimately, ritual leaders as human beings can never help another to find complete wholeness and healing. Praying for those for whom we are caring for, in our own time and space, may help us maintain a healthy perspective of our role and limitations, and also give us a means of letting go of the bereaved and their deceased loved ones into God's care. Cooper-White (2004, 191), from within the context of pastoral care and counselling, puts it this way:

When we pray for those who come to us for (pastoral) care or counseling, we find ourselves more able to relinquish the heroic need to rescue. We are restored to the recognition that healing and wholeness come from God, not our own interventions, and that God's love is vast enough to contain all the suffering that is beyond human efforts to save.

Care of the spiritual dimension of another is informed by a range of approaches or tools garnered from secular psychotherapeutic methods – such the utilisation of Carl Roger's (1967) concepts of empathy, congruence and unconditional regard or the development of Freud's ideas of transference and counter-transference within therapeutic relationships (Cooper-White 2004). Such resources are not merely glibly gleaned and utilised by church representatives without thought

64

but require theological critique before being adopted for practice. For example, Roger's therapeutic triad may be deemed helpful to adopt within the context of a spiritual care relationship but the absence within his approach of encouraging clients to engage with ethical frames of reference out with their own intuitive sense of right and wrong may not resonate sympathetically with a theologically informed approach. In this respect spiritual care is always more than applied psychology.

For a church representative providing spiritual care that which fundamentally shapes, forms and reforms her personhood and motivation for involvement in caring for the bereaved – her beliefs and participation in Christian worship, prayer and theological reflection – is the same in any caring relationship. She is fundamentally the same person in providing person-centred spiritual care, pastoral care and, where appropriate, spiritual direction. In caring relationships where the carer's theology, personhood and identity is shaped by the Christian metanarrative, how she makes herself available and how she relates to another is of significance in sharing Christ's love (Kelly 2007). In all forms of care, she offers the same quality of relationship but in offering person–centred spiritual care the Christian story and the resources it offers are not explicitly utilised as a means to help structure or reinterpret the particular story or set of circumstances of another. Essentially, the manner in which all forms of care are offered and what informs that manner are the same: the quality of the relationship formed and the way of relating to and being with another is central to providing sensitive care of the spiritual dimension as the church representative seeks to embody the compassion of Christ in supporting the bereaved.

5

Co-constructing Funerals

Introduction to Ritual

Rituals are deliberate, detailed, and repeated patterns of activity that are infused with multiple meanings. . . . They are potent means of symbolic expression, have a strong affective component, and can be either privately created and enacted or the shared products of culture.

Romanoff and Thompson (2006, 313)

A funeral is a culturally shaped ritual which has the potential to enable the enactment of specific relationships and the retelling, and perhaps the reinterpretation, of particular stories in light of the narratives or grand narrative informing those who helped to construct and share in the ritual. In the bereaved's search to make sense of their experience of loss and relationship with the deceased the process of ritualising their loved one's life and death is highly significant, as 'Ritual is a symbol system aimed at the product and dissemination of meaning' (Anderson and Foley 1998–9, 18). Such meaning may be both corporate and individual (Froggatt 1997).

In the throes of bereavement, we come face to face with trying to make sense of the mystery of death. It can raise deep questions in us such as what our life is about. It has always seemed natural to me to explore ritual as a way of coming to terms with what has happened.

Often rituals at such time involve what at face value may seem fairly mundane activities; the placing of flowers on a

66

grave, saying a prayer in the garden, putting pictures of loved ones in frames. These are all familiar and universal ritual acts.

Much of our lives involve mundane routine activities like sleeping, working, travelling and eating. However, we can choose to imbue life with significance and meaning through imagination, ritual and acts of connectedness with others. The role of ritual appears deeply rooted in the imagination and the will. Through our will and imagination, we bring the significance of ritual into being. (Arthacharya 2005, 35)

The difference between a ritual and a routine act is that which is invested in it. For example, a candle lit specifically to mark the anniversary of a loved one's death may have vastly different meanings than the regular lighting of a candle to enhance the ambience of a family mealtime.

Traditionally, major life transitions, such as childbirth, marriage and death have been marked by rituals known as 'rites of passage', a phrase developed by the French anthropologist Arnold van Gennep (1960 [1908]). As his reflections on rites of passage developed van Gennep proposed that each ritual had a similar tripartite form and contained elements which 'symbolically and practically signify change from one state to another' (Froggatt 1997, 45). The three aspects or phases the bereaved have to live through, contained within the ritual process of marking the life and death of a significant other, according to van Gennep are as follows.

Pre-liminal (Separating) Phase
In this phase, symbolic behaviour signifying detachment from the cultural and social norms of a living person is performed by the bereaved, for example, seeing the deceased's body, collecting his clothes and possessions from his last place of care, selecting a coffin and writing a death notice for a newspaper.

Liminal (Transition) Phase

In this second phase, the bereaved are in an ambiguous state. They are in a period of limbo – neither as they were prior to bereavement nor as they shall be once they have accommodated the experience of grief into their lives and way of living. This phase may be initiated by involvement in one of a myriad of ritual moments before, during and after the funeral when the bereaved feel confronted with the reality of the death of their loved one.[1] Such a period may last for many months and is marked by feelings of disorientation, anxiety and difficulty in living life with a sense of normality or fulfilment. It is a time of waiting which has to be lived with and through; the length of this phase is not under conscious control.

Post-liminal (Reaggregating) Phase

In this final phase, the rite of passage is concluded and the bereaved are perceived to act and relate once again in accordance with familial and societal norms. The bereaved may continue to ritually remember their loved one (e.g., by looking through old photographs or the contents of a memory box) following reaggregation into full community life without the stigma of bereavement but expressed emotion focussed around such ongoing ritual activity is transitory.

The deceased may also be thought of as going through such a tripartite process. First, the separation at death from loved ones. Second, the liminal phase of resting in a mortuary or funeral director's premises (and/or, more rarely now, in their own home) between their death and disposal. Finally, the deceased's funeral marks their entering into the post-liminal phase when they are buried or cremated and their ashes then disposed of.

---

1   This process of ritualising the life and death of a significant other is described more fully below.

Funerals in Ritual Context

Death is 'a momentous occurrence with an impact on the
entire group (to which the dying person belongs), which
solemnises it with rituals and public ceremonies. An individual death (in this context) is never trivial since it splits
open the treasury of myths and symbols of the community'.
Bouwsma (1998, 190 [citing Gonzalez-Crussi 1993, 168])

The premise of this book is that funerals, and the manner in
which they are constructed, may help to meet some of the
myriad of psychological, social, spiritual and practical needs
that a bereaved individual, family or community may have
following the death of a cherished person. As Bouwsma suggests, the impact of a death on a network of social relations is
significant and requires a way in which what has been, what
currently is and what may be can be acknowledged. However,
it is not only during a funeral that a person's life and death is
ritually marked. A funeral is a formal ritual moment, albeit a
highly significant one, within a process of ritualising which
takes place over a lengthy period following the death of a loved
one.[2] The following list provides some of the formal and
informal ritual moments or actions which bereaved individuals may choose to perform themselves and/or share in with
others after a death.

---

2 Ritual is an important part of preparation for an expected death and also takes the
form of a process involving informal and more formal ritual moments depending
on the individuals and community concerned. Such a process begins when bad
news about a diagnosis or prognosis is anticipated and may extend over a period
of time. It may involve such actions as a dying individual making out a will, putting his or her financial affairs in order, writing letters or making cards for family
members to open at significant milestones or creating memory boxes in which
are placed important items for surviving loved ones to have and to aid their
future reminiscing. More formal religious ritual moments may be shared, according
to the dying person's particular faith tradition, for example, being anointed or
receiving the Sacrament of the Sick.

Pre-funeral Rituals

- Being present at a loved one's expected death (where possible).[3]
- Seeing and spending time with the deceased (and perhaps doing so more than once either in the institution where they died or in the funeral director's premises).
- Helping to wash\lay out and dress the deceased.
- Collecting the death certificate and belongings of the deceased from the institution where they died.
- Registering the death.
- Meeting with a funeral director to arrange practicalities of the funeral.[4]
- Choosing appropriate clothes (or a simple shroud) for the deceased to wear, selecting objects or photographs and perhaps writing letters to, or drawing or painting pictures for, the deceased (to be placed in the coffin).
- Preparing an appropriately worded death notice for the local and/or national newspaper.
- Meeting with the church representative sharing in the funeral and co-constructing the ritual and all that this involves – from telling the story of the deceased and his/her relationship with them, negotiating the content of the funeral with other family members and the ritual leader to finalising the practical arrangements.
- Visits from friends, neighbours and church members to the bereaved and the sharing of stories about the deceased.

---

3 Being present when a loved one dies unexpectedly, especially in traumatic circumstances would not be an action which would be invested with the same kind of meaning as choosing to be present (where possible) at the death of someone whose death has been expected and prepared for.

4 Linked with this ritual activity are other associated informal ritual moments such as choosing floral tributes and an appropriate coffin, selecting the mode and place of disposal of the deceased and deciding how the body and the mourners will be transported, choosing an appropriate establishment for the post-funeral gathering and often through the funeral director approaching a representative of the church or other celebrant to help perform the funeral.

- Being present if the coffin is placed in the church or in the family home for the night before the funeral.
- The deceased's last journey from his home to place of disposal accompanied by family and close friends.

Post-funeral Rituals
- Wake or post funeral refreshments associated with further reminiscing about life shared with the deceased.
- Writing letters and phoning distant friends and family to inform them of a loved one's death.
- Disposal of ashes – scattering or burying.
- Dealing with the deceased's estate.
- Answering sympathy cards and acknowledging flowers and support received.
- Informing banks, utility companies and local and national government agencies of loved one's death.
- Clearing out of deceased's home and dispersing their belongings.
- Ordering of a headstone for a grave or a plaque to be placed within the crematorium grounds, choosing wording for the memorial and visiting it for first time.

Ongoing Ritual Remembering
- Visiting place of disposal and tending grave.
- Planting a tree, shrub or bush and watching it change through the seasons and over the years.
- Purchasing a seat or bench in a place significant to the deceased and visiting specifically to remember or share important news or decision-making.
- Informal rituals in own home, for example, looking at contents of a memory box containing photographs and letters from the deceased, lighting a candle on significant days or putting special ornaments on the Christmas tree in memory of the deceased.
- Creating and visiting virtual memorials (available on the web).

- Sharing experiences and feelings with others online via websites designed specifically for the bereaved.[5]
- Participating in memorial services or times of remembrance organised by families, churches or caring institutions such as hospitals or hospices.
- Publicly marking the anniversary of the death or birthday of a deceased loved one by making an entry into the *In memoriam* column of a newspaper.[6]
- Continuing to share stories about the deceased which may be stimulated by participating in any of the above ritual means of remembering.

Much may be invested in ritual moments which may be initiated and facilitated by the bereaved themselves or in dialogue with family members, friends or caring professionals supporting them. Such rituals and others which are particular to individuals or families evolve from the needs and experience of those living with the loss and what is considered appropriate within the social matrix which they inhabit. For example, one father following the death of his baby had her name tattooed on his arm alongside the names of his partner and parents. As well as aiding the recall of memories associated with the deceased one significant reason why such rituals are performed is summed up by this grieving parent: *'It shows how much she means to us.'* (Father 5) The variety of different nuances as to what these various acts of remembering mean are highly subjective and are dependent on the relationship of the bereaved

---

5   For example in the United Kingdom the website www.rd4U.org.uk which is designed for bereaved teenagers as part of the services Cruse Bereavement Care offer.

6   This may continue for many years and like all rituals will be informed by the story and circumstances of the grieving family no matter at what stage in life their loved one died.

with the deceased as well as their own individual, family and community history of dealing with death.

Tom Gordon (2006, 120), a former parish minister and now a hospice chaplain based in Edinburgh, notes a change in the pattern of ritualising death in Scottish urban culture in his working lifetime spanning over 30 years:

> People don't close their curtains or lower their blinds any more to indicate if there has been a death in their house or their street. The cremation has largely taken the place of the graveside burial. Corteges are less common in the cities now, with the hearse often waiting at the crematorium gates or the coffin even being in place in the crematorium chapel before the mourners arrive. People choose to have their loved one 'viewed' at the funeral director's rest rooms and less frequently at home. Men don't doff their hats as a hearse drives by. Seldom would people come back to the house for a wake, choosing instead to go onto a hotel for a more formal gathering for refreshments.

Although there may have been a loss of some of the rituals of yesteryear associated with death, other rituals have emerged which have become significant in their own way in our more fragmented society where we communicate increasingly more readily through cyberspace than verbally with those next door – such as creating a virtual memoriam and making virtual pilgrimages of remembrance to it or entering into supportive relationships with other bereaved persons online. These and the rituals of creating floral roadside shrines at the scene of a fatal traffic accident, the mass lighting of candles, the releasing of helium balloons and the dispersal of a loved one's ashes on a hill or mountain top are our new cultural norms in response to death in our local and global communities.

Process of Co-constructing Funerals

> We need a ceremony that, in the midst of relatives and
> friends, allows us to express our gratitude for the ones we
> have lost and mourn their passing. (Holloway 2005, 11)

At its lowest common denominator, having a funeral is a
dignified and respectful, as well as hygienic, way to dispose of
any human body. Even if the deceased was not particularly
loved, liked or virtuous in life, a funeral is deemed an appropriate civilised act to be performed in order to mark the life and
death of an individual in contemporary Western culture.
Arranging and ensuring a funeral is conducted is considered to
be a moral obligation on the part of society, a duty usually
undertaken by the family, if there is one, or by the local authority if not. At a basic level, a funeral is performed because the
deceased is human, as opposed to bovine, porcine or equine.

Several years ago in Craigmillar, a large housing estate in
Edinburgh, a newborn baby was found dead and abandoned
on some waste ground. Neither the baby's mother nor father
was ever traced. However, the whole community took ownership of the baby and rallied round to raise money to pay for the
funeral which the local parish minister performed and many
attended. A unique human being had lived, albeit briefly, and
died who needed to be respectfully laid to rest in a culturally
appropriate way.

A funeral is both for the deceased and the bereaved, being a
key formal ritual act within a process of the ongoing marking
of the significance of a unique person's life and death. 'Funerals
are important since they mark the passing of a human being
from the society of the living to the world of the dead. Death is
a passage which the funeral formalises' (Sheppy 2003, 78). A
funeral also has an important role in enabling the grieving of
those left behind to be facilitated – both in terms of beginning
to acknowledge the reality of death and letting go as well as
paradoxically helping the bereaved to integrate the deceased's

life and death into their evolving story. However, it is not just attending and participating in a funeral that can significantly impact on the well-being of the recently bereaved, the manner in which the funeral is constructed also potentially affects their grieving. If the bereaved choose to be involved with the ritual leader in co-authoring the funeral, they are not only marking change but are also actively owning and making change – 'people select images and practices which help them manage their loss, and as they do so they construct ritual' (Hockey 2001 cited by Stoddart 2006, 33). Following the death of a significant other, enabling a bereaved individual or family to participate in co-constructing the funeral, enhances the likelihood of a more relevant and authentic ritual to be shared. The essence of giving the bereaved the opportunity to co-create a funeral for their loved one is about empowering them at a time of great vulnerability and distress and not about controlling or containing their grief and ritual marking.

Evidence from recent research carried out with bereaved parents who helped to co-create their baby's funeral will be utilised to underpin this argument, as well as reference to examples from hospice chaplaincy practice. By referring to parental perceptions of their experience, the potential therapeutic benefits to the bereaved of such an approach to creating funerals will be explored. However, before doing so, the way in which a church representative may approach the process of co-constructing a funeral with a bereaved family will be outlined.

A Ritual Evolves Over Time

The days and weeks following even an expected death can be a highly confusing and disorientating time for the bereaved. First, it is vital when co-constructing funerals with bereaved relatives to give them permission to take time to reflect on the content and form of a funeral in the days following the death of a significant other. Second, it is important for the ritual leader to make time and space not just to allow the bereaved to tell and retell their stories as they try to make sense of what has happened but also to enable the church representative to re-iterate and repeat the options available to the bereaved and to allow them to reflect on the decisions they tentatively make. A funeral should never be simply pieced together during a one-off encounter between ritual leader and a family, unless for their own reasons they wish it so. Memories and shared moments, feelings and pieces of prose, poetry and music are recollected which may be utilised during the ritual not just within the context of a meeting with a church representative in a living room or chaplain's office. The initial encounter between the bereaved and the ritual leader may spark off further reminiscing and reflection by family members, both collectively and individually, so potentially new ideas are called to mind over time which may be incorporated. Furthermore, families require their own time and space to make decisions regarding the funeral arrangements, its content and who might, in particular, participate in verbalising or acting out their rela-tionship with the deceased during the funeral, for example sharing some personal reflections or placing a flower in the grave or carrying the coffin. Thus, during a first meeting with a bereaved family the ritual leader should make a firm arrange-ment to be in contact again with them, either in person, by telephone or (as last resort) e-mail, to finalise the funeral prior to the day of the ritual. Ideally, the bereaved should also feel free in the interim to be in touch with the church representa-tive, should they have any questions, change their minds about funeral content, require further information or need someone to talk things through to clarify their decision-making or lessen their fears and anxieties.

Listening to Stories
Of self

Gerkin (1984, 27), in an exploration of what is the essence of offering pastoral counselling, says this:

The pastoral counsellor is not only a listener to stories; he is also a bearer of stories and a story. The pastoral counsellor does not come empty-handed to the task of understanding the other's story and offering the possibility of a new interpretation. The pastoral counsellor brings his own interpretation of life experience with its use of commonly held symbols, images, and themes from the cultural milieu of the counsellor, and the private, nuanced meanings that have been shaped by the pastoral counsellor's own life experience and private interpretation.

In seeking to work with a family to create a relevant funeral a ritual leader is not engaged in the kind of intensive ongoing contractual and highly structured relationship that is pastoral counselling. Nevertheless, what Gerkin says of the pastoral counsellor as someone who carries stories with her into a counselling relationship as well as listening to the stories of a client resonates with what is true of a ritual leader seeking to co-construct ritual with the bereaved. In an encounter where a church representative offers spiritual care following the death of an individual, she not only listens to, and interprets, the stories of the bereaved but she also embodies and lives out a multiplicity of stories as she relates to them. Prior to entering into such a relationship with bereaved persons, a church representative must have a reasonable awareness of her own story and the multiple stories, including the grand narrative, which informs it. A ritual leader's interpretation of the Christian story, her theology, shapes her practice of providing spiritual care which includes her way of relating and acting out the divine story. In addition, her theology also informs what she considers the role of a funeral to be, her role in its construction and performance and whom she feels owns the funeral and, thus, controls its content. These are key questions for any spiritual carer to consider before seeking to work with the bereaved and share in ritual construction and its performance. It is important that the ritual leader is open and honest about her theology and approach to ritual construction, its content and performance and makes her position clear to the bereaved when they approach her for assistance, especially if the bereaved family do not know her well. This enables both the family and the church representative to decide whether they want to enter into the important relationship out of which the funeral is constructed. Moreover, reflecting theologically on the experience of creating funerals and sharing in them with families is significant for informing ongoing practice. Such considerations are at the heart of this book.

The bereaved themselves will invest their own meaning in the ritual leader as a person of authority and a representative of God and the church (and any institution she works in). Again, it is of importance that ritual leaders are aware of the possibilities of this happening and are sensitive to such transference and projection, if and when, they become aware of it.

Of others

Following the death of a loved one, the bereaved have a plethora of spiritual needs, including a desire to express their feelings, beliefs and experience in a manner which is relevant and meaningful to them. The rediscovery of the importance of ritual in our postmodern world is key as to how such needs can be best met, at least in part, communally and individually. Within our present-day context where the formation of worldviews and the making of decisions are based on personal understanding and reflection on experience rather than deference to external authorities (Heelas and Woodhead 2005) or grand narratives, church representatives have to take seriously the stories of the bereaved they seek to support and work with. At the heart of enabling the co-construction of funerals with bereaved families is that which is essential to providing any spiritual care; namely, beginning where they are in their grief and life's journey and being attentive to their particular story. Furthermore, the ritual leader involved not only is required to relate to the bereaved as a 'living human document'; a sacred text worthy of time and attention which needs interpretation and understanding (Bennett Moore 2002, 17 with reference to work of the ground-breaking American pastoral theologian/chaplain Anton Boisen). She, in order to help co-construct a funeral appropriate to the particular needs perceived, also requires some understanding of the context in which grief is expressed. Feminist pastoral theologians helpfully refer to this as reading the 'living human web' (Bennett Moore 2002, 17 citing Miller-McLemore 1996, 14); the cultural and social background in which particular individuals and families experience bereavement. James (2004, 59) emphasises how important such an approach is:

> The clergy have a key role in making arrangements for funerals and it is important for them to understand what is happening in the community, be it large or small. The funeral is not the property of the Church but a ritual in which the whole of society has a role to play.

Meaningful funerals emerge from the interaction between the story of the deceased as retold by the grieving family and the story of the church representative and all that informs both narratives.[7] Romanoff and Thompson (2006, 313) helpfully reflect on such ritual formation developing out of narrative engagement between a dying patient and a health care professional:

> It is important to note that the design and enactment of rituals is a cocreation of the patient and practitioner and not a stock exercise. As in all narratives, the symbolic meanings emerge from the intersubjective creative act and cannot be externally imposed.

---

7   Some people who are dying may have chosen to plan their funeral before their death with or without the aid of other family members or a ritual leader and may have left specific instructions. However, any funeral is not simply for the deceased. It is also for the bereaved and such instructions need to be revisited and discussed after the death to explore their possible implications for those attending.

In the context of pastoral care, the stories of the deceased and the bereaved and their relationship(s) may be reinterpreted in light of the Christian metanarrative. However, in the twenty-first century where many bereaved have no knowledge of this grand narrative, utilisation of the language, stories and images of the Christian faith by the church representative during a funeral is inappropriate and much of the ritual performed may be meaningless.

> For better or worse bereavement care (including the co-creation of funerals)[8] now concerns not dogmatic avowals of faith in the resurrection but a real engagement with an individual's story. (Murray 2002, 136)

It is the perceptions, worldviews and stories of the bereaved and the deceased that require articulating and enacting within the funeral, not the ritual leaders. The funeral belongs not to the individual managing it but to those who mourn. Construction of ritual is ideally done through a 'partnership' (Carr 1985, 111) which the church representative seeks to establish with the bereaved. During the funeral itself she often, though not always, acts on their behalf. Therefore, the ritual leader has to risk utilising language, images and metaphors learnt from the bereaved and their world, as well as from her tradition (when appropriate), as she seeks to enable the deceased's story to be retold, reinterpreted and reenacted within the wider context of the family, human, and divine stories (in relation to the mysteries of life, death and what may be beyond) in a manner that is relevant and comprehensible.[9]

Sharing Cultural Norms

Walter (1994) suggests the postmodern approach to dealing with death and bereavement perceives the professional as no

---

8   My words in parentheses not Murray's.
9   How a church representative may do this with theological integrity is discussed in the next chapter.

longer the considered expert; the dying and bereaved set the agenda. The professional involved listens and learns. However, the carer may need to offer images and a language to aid the individual concerned to express himself/herself as well as information to enable him to choose to do things his way (should this be his need). In the postmodern world, the terminally ill may not know how to die nor the bereaved how to grieve for as well as there no longer being a shared metanarrative to aid an exploration of questions of meaning associated with suffering, life and death, our Western society is also bereft of cultural norms to inform our grieving. In addition, there are fewer commonly held ritual norms following a death (Murray 2002). For some this can be liberating if they are confident enough to grieve in their own particular way without feeling the overwhelming need to conform to other's expectations. They can also ritually mark the life and death of a significant other in a manner they consider appropriate without feeling hypocritical in utilising, or being constrained by, an alien religious liturgy or cultic actions.

However, there is no doubt that present-day society is in a state of flux regarding how we ritually deal with death, potentially leading to further uncertainty and confusion in the minds of many bereaved persons at an already disorientating time. What are appropriate and relevant choices to make regarding rituals, especially a funeral, which are not only culturally acceptable but also personally helpful? How can the bereaved find benchmarks to enable comparisons and, thus, inform decision-making regarding funeral arrangements, and content and form, especially if they have never dealt with the death of a significant other before? This is where the process of a church representative working with a family to co-construct a meaningful funeral has a significant role to play. The ritual leader is not only required to listen intently to the bereaved sharing their stories of grief but she also has a role in empowering the bereaved to make informed choices. This involves sharing relevant information regarding practicalities concerned with the funeral and its planning as well as, from experience, the possible scenarios and implications of choosing certain options open to them. One example of this may involve talking through the pros and cons of a burial for a particular family compared to a cremation when the deceased has not informed their family of their wishes regarding the disposal of their body.

Offering the means to articulate and act out stories and relationships

In a postmodern setting where the majority of bereaved relatives or their deceased or dying loved one has or had no contact with a faith community, a common associated comment made along with tentative enquiry as to whether a church representative will perform the funeral is – 'He wasn't religious.' or 'She wouldn't have wanted anything too religious. She didn't go to church.' In such cases, the chaplain or parish church worker may be seen 'more as a friend and companion than a religious official' (Murray 2002, 26). On further gentle exploration, even though there has not been any church connection nor any particular orthodox Christian beliefs held, there still may be a strong feeling that a hymn or hymns (those requested are often ones sung at other family funerals or are familiar from childhood) should be sung, perhaps a prayer said and their deceased loved one committed into God's eternal love and care. Frequently, the offer of the contact details of a local Humanist celebrant are declined when an explanation is given that the aforementioned constituents of more traditional funerals would not be permitted as part of a Humanist funeral. The reply often comes that the bereaved do not mind such components as long as 'religion isn't laid on too thick' or 'we don't want God not to be included' or 'he believed in God but not in the church, so not churchy stuff'. van Tongeren (2004, 137), a Dutch Roman Catholic liturgist, helpfully comments on this increasing separation of belief from the institutional church:

> The personalized funeral appears to hang together with
> the privatization and individualization that are character-
> istic of the lifestyle and thinking in postmodern culture,
> which distance themselves from institutional forms of
> religion. . . . Not what a church believes, but the personal
> relationship with God is central.

The dying and bereaved also frequently make it clear that
they'd rather someone they knew, or at least knew of shared in
their funeral rather than a complete stranger (e.g., a healthcare
chaplain from the nursing staff or in the case of a church representative working in a parish setting from neighbours or
through attending another rite of passage which she had participated in).

As an aid to enabling the patients and relatives I work with to
articulate their longings and lament, hopes and fears, questions
and thanksgiving, I offer them a portfolio of sacred and secular
texts from which they may want to select something suitable
for the funeral. This takes the form of an eclectic selection of
biblical readings, poems, prose, prayers and blessings from
a variety of sources and eras which other bereaved persons have
found helpful, or indeed have actually written. They can keep
such a resource at their bedside or take it home to peruse.

It is interesting to note that some bereaved persons who are
not believers, or are rather not unbelievers, for whom sacred
texts do not play a significant part in their lives or worldview,
do choose biblical passages or poems with religious themes or
motifs to be read or hymns to be sung. For example, psalms
of lament or readings such as 1 Corinthians 13 and Ecclesiastes
3: 1–8 are utilised as pieces of literature with timeless sentiment,
rather than as sacred texts, which speak to their situation and
articulate their feelings or wrestling. Such inherited utterances
may help untangle something of the otherwise unspeakable,
indefinable or incomprehensible, at a time when their own
words prove elusive. As Steinke (2006, 340) puts it: 'Literary

resources provide the language we need when pain and suffering destroy language.'

The bereaved will often have specific ideas for music to be
played or hymns to be sung (sometimes at the deceased's
request) before, during and after the funeral in the crematorium or church. Much time and energy is spent in choosing
these key elements in any rite of passage. The church representative will be asked for guidance by some, certain songs, hymns
and pieces of music may be run by the ritual leader, though
increasingly families will simply bypass any veto by a ritual
leader. However decisions are reached, music is significant
to any funeral. 'Music, in its many forms and for all kinds of
reasons, can reach the aching void within. It can touch inner
sensibilities that are too deep, too inchoate and too painful to
be expressed in words'(Deyner 1997, 200).

It is also helpful to describe various ways in which family
members or friends and former colleagues can actively participate in the funeral itself, or its preparation, if they wish.
However, this has to be done sensitively so as not create the
impression that any of these activities is a prescribed cultural
norm which has to be adhered to and, thus, potentially another
decision to make or burden to bear at time which may be confusing and stressful enough already. Do they wish to carry the
coffin into the crematorium or lower it into the grave? Do
they wish themselves to place anything on the coffin during
the funeral and/or throw flowers, earth or petals onto the
coffin during a burial? Do children or grandchildren, who may
or may not be present, wish to draw or paint pictures for the
deceased which might decorate or be put in the coffin? Have
the family thought about flowers for the funeral (and who
might source and/or arrange them – perhaps a member of the
family or a friend is a keen gardener or flower arranger) or a
retiring collection as a gesture of love? Does anyone from the
family or deceased's circle of friends want to say anything, sing
or play an instrument during the funeral? If not, do they want
to write something that might be read out? How do they feel

about a time of silence in which everyone can have their own thoughts about the deceased or say their own silent prayers?[10] Would anyone in the family like to design and print out an order of service for the funeral?

Reviewing

After the ritual leader has listened to the stories of the bereaved, assessed their ritual needs, shared a range of resources and suggested possible ritual actions, it may well be time in the encounter to review what has been shared. As part of my own practice, both as an aide memoir and as a means of helping to structure my note taking, I utilise a checklist of issues I feel are important to be raised during the process of co-construction of a funeral.[11] Furthermore, to help move things forward it may now be appropriate to outline a possible framework within which the content of the funeral could be structured. Such a suggested order for the funeral is informed not just by the family's needs but also by the ritual leader's experience, theology and the religious tradition to which she belongs. The intention here is not to finalise what will be done and said but to open a dialogue as to what form the funeral will take. Again, this is a consultative process and not an imposition of a 'prayer book' liturgy. It is important that the ritual leader explains why she is suggesting a certain order and that what she is putting forward is for negotiation and discussion, as and when required. This is an area in which the bereaved especially feel lost and do appreciate a short explanation of the reasons, theological and practical, why a funeral might be ordered in a particular way. They may have an idea of the general 'feel' that they want for the funeral or even know the specific things they want said, sung or done but seldom do they know in what order.

---

10 This can also be a helpful way of making an otherwise non-religious funeral more inclusive for those attending who, whether they have Christian beliefs or not, wish to pray.

11 See appendix 1.

After such a review and hopefully coming to an agreement of the order of the funeral, if not finalising the content, it is helpful to ask the family if they have any other questions and importantly if they feel content with what has been discussed and is being proposed. This gives the family an opportunity to raise anxieties or concerns about the funeral and the manner in which it will be performed. At this point, both the family and the ritual leader still have the opportunity to withdraw from the relationship if either party feels uncomfortable about each other's needs or stated requirements. The church representative may be able to refer the family to a colleague, a ritual leader from another faith community, to an interfaith or Humanist celebrant or to the funeral director who could do likewise.

Dealing with Practicalities

It is as important for the ritual leader as well as the bereaved that a conversation about the practicalities of the funeral is initiated. Confirming the time and place of the funeral as well as the bereaved's expectation of where the church representative will meet them prior to its commencement is fundamental. Some families will wish the ritual leader to say a prayer in their home before they leave for the funeral, though this is rarer in Scotland than it used to be, especially as fewer deceased persons are brought home the night before the funeral. More commonly, the ritual leader will meet the family where the funeral is to take place. It should be stated clearly how long the funeral should last, especially if it is being held in a crematorium, so the family are aware of the boundaries of time as well as space.[12] If family members and friends are actively

---

12   If family members have not previously visited or yet chosen the setting of their loved one's funeral suggesting they do visit may reduce the number of unknowns for them on the day of the ritual and may help them make informed choices for the funeral. This especially is of significance if the deceased or the bereaved have decided on a burial and family members may be returning to visit the grave. If the funeral is taking place in a crematorium which they have never been in, it is of help to describe the crematorium or refer the family to a booklet or website where photographs may be viewed.

participating in the ritual through word, song, instrumental playing, silence or ritual action it should be clarified, after prior negotiation, when this will happen, where, how and for how long. In particular, if more than one person is involved in sharing memories or reminisces of the deceased it should be made clear who is talking about what and for what length of time, to avoid repetition and the funeral overrunning.

Even if it is only the ritual leader herself who is conducting the funeral with communal involvement restricted to singing, reflection in silence and the opportunity to make a donation to a retiring collection, the practicalities of the service should be run through and checked out with the family.

After confirmation, at a later date, of the funeral's content and structure with the bereaved family, contact with the funeral director and crematorium staff and/or church officer, organist and appropriate members is required to communicate the family's specific wishes and ensure appropriate arrangements are in place.

Sharing in the Co-construction and Performance of Funerals – Meeting the Needs of the Bereaved

It is all too easy for those of us who are immersed in working with bereaved families to assume that we know what needs we are meeting and how. We often receive a polite thank you and a handshake at the end of the ritual and maybe a handwritten note or card and sometimes a gesture of thanks, such as a book token or bottle. Much as these tokens of gratitude are appreciated, do we really know if we are meeting peoples' real needs (and not just our assumed perception of them) and helping them in their grief by the manner we approach ritual construction and performance? As a hospital chaplain supporting bereaved parents, I felt I was doing reasonably well in this regard but I had no real evidence. My colleagues and I all worked in a similar way (outlined above) to seek to co-author funerals with bereaved parents, whether they described themselves as religious or not. Therefore, to satisfy my curiosity I decided to reflect on our practice by asking a small cohort of 25 parents (involved in 13 funerals for their babies) with whom my four colleagues had worked, for their perceptions of their experience of bereavement and working with a chaplain to co-construct and share in their baby's funeral.[13] The remainder of this chapter and part of the next contains themes which emerged from analysis of the narratives shared by the bereaved parents during in-depth interviews. Their experience shows how significant funerals which have been 'created and designed inductively' (van Tongeren 2004, 134) are in meeting the spiritual, psychological, social and practical needs of the bereaved.

Meeting Spiritual Needs

Co-construction of funerals enables:

Development of a relationship of trust between church representative and the bereaved. Parents described antici-pating meeting a chaplain for the first time after their child's death as an anxiety-provoking experience, even for those who felt some affiliation with the church.[14] *'I expected a lot more awk-wardness.'* (Father 7)[15] Church representatives were not only expected to actively proselytise but also to be indifferent to, and detached from, the distress and pain of parental grief. *'I was just expecting him to come in and say what he had to say and go'* (Mother 7). Parents also assumed that the chaplain would offer purely religious support which not only would be inappropri-ate but also would not be concerned with meeting their real needs. *'A preconceived idea that this is a strictly religious or very religious, over the top religious, offering'* (Father 13).

---

13   The demography of the 25 parents involved in the qualitative study can be found in appendix 2.

14   Of the 25 parents interviewed only 1 was actively involved in a local faith com-munity, 11 described themselves as having some non-active affiliation with the church and 13 described themselves as having no affiliation whatsoever.

15   See appendix 2 for demographic details.

By spending time with the bereaved and developing relationships with them as they sought to create appropriate funerals for their babies, church representatives helped to dispel some of the negative expectations parents had of them. *'He showed us that he was a person. He is not the religious; put him on a pedestal type'* (Father 6). Moreover, at a time of great vulnerability the bereaved felt a real need of support from trusted others and by the approach of making themselves available and listening to parent's particular stories chaplains were able to fulfil such a role. *'Even though we had only met her briefly it was almost like an old friend and we needed her'* (Father 12).

The articulation of the need for such a relationship between a church representative and the bereaved underlines David Stoter's (1995, 8) assertion that:

> in order to be able to offer spiritual care at all, the carer must be acceptable to the person receiving the care . . . moving onto deeper levels needs a caring relationship or contract to be firmly established where the recipient can accept the carer as someone who can be entrusted with all their needs, hopes and fears, pains and distresses and to whom they can entrust themselves fully and totally.

The process of co-construction enables the bereaved and the ritual leader to have the opportunity to develop the type of relationship where assumptions might be cast aside, acceptance offered and received, and trust established. Thus, creating an appropriate context within which survivors can be themselves and express their needs openly, rather than feel subdued or disempowered by the church representative's perceived ritual authority. The establishment of such a relationship enhances the possibility of a ritual leader and bereaved family working creatively and coherently together. The bereaveds' spiritual, psychological, social and practical needs are best assessed and met within such a relationship of trust, where even within a short period of time intimate and troubling aspects of their stories may be shared and concerns about the implications of various aspects of ritual aired. Such a relationship resonates with the biblical notion of a covenant, a relationship based on trust where the carer's concerns are centred on the quality of relationship formed and the needs of the whole person rather than on seeking the other to conform to a certain set of behaviours or a relationship which is primarily of benefit to the carer (Pembroke 2002). Significantly for the bereaved, having the opportunity to develop a sense of the ritual leader's approach and humanity, as well as professional capabilities, during co-construction, helped to reduce concern about further interaction with her and the subsequent funeral which developed from such engagement. The importance of developing such trust in the ritual leader prior to the funeral is highlighted by Ainsworth-Smith and Speck (1999, 99):

> Many bereaved people are frightened by the intensity of their feelings, and the presence of other people whom they trust, coupled with a sensitive and calm leadership of the ritual, can enable them to feel safe about expressing feelings at the funeral.

Meaningful funerals.   Parents did not remember all, indeed, sometimes very little of what was said during their baby's funeral but they certainly could articulate the general feel of the ritual. The overall sense of parents was that the process of co-construction enabled the funeral to be grounded in the reality of their experience, feelings and beliefs. *'she addressed our individual and personal wants shall we say . . . she didn't fit the pre-conceived bill if you know what I mean . . . of what I had, and what we, thought was going to be a massive religious service'* (Father 13). What was said during rituals reflected what had been shared with the chaplain during co-construction – through the poems, readings and prayers either parents or chaplains had chosen or written, and/or by the chaplains' weaving of the family's story into the ritual. *'It was all true and to the point'* (Father 7).

Furthermore, parents appreciated that what had been said and shared was not a set or given liturgy but that time and trouble had been taken to create something particular and special for their unique loved one. 'In the utilisation of denominational liturgies or "prayer book" funerals ... stories from scripture or religious tradition can often be imposed on people's experience in a way that denies them an authentic voice' (Lynch and Willows 2000, 182–3). It is important when working with the bereaved to co-create a funeral which respects and reflects their stories and that of their deceased loved one.

Not only do authentic funerals affirm and validate the bereaved's experience and feelings but they also aid them in their meaning-making. *'Today was about celebrating what we had. I think acknowledging that was very important and I guess that contributed to a feeling of uplift.'* (Mother 1 talking about the fact that, for her, having her baby in her life, albeit for a short time, was meaningful and significant. This was a cause for thanksgiving and she appreciated the fact that this was reflected in her baby's funeral.) Anderson and Foley (1998–9, 18) eloquently highlight the significance of this: 'The power of ritual to communicate meaning ... is diminished when the ritual is dishonest or contradicts clear experience.'

Parents expressed their surprise and appreciation that the chaplain used ordinary, everyday language during the funerals, as well referring to their baby and other family members by their preferred or pet names.

One important aspect of co-creation which greatly helps to personalise a funeral is enabling the bereaved to choose music, sacred or secular, which for them encapsulates the situation, the life of the deceased and their relationship with him. Listening, for example, to the music which a mother played for her baby while in her womb or that a couple danced to while they courted and at their wedding or the tune played at their football team's

stadium every home game[16] is important if such music is identified with the deceased by those present. Hymns sung at
funerals are often part of family tradition and not having them
at a member's funeral would be unthinkable, whether they
were firm believers or not.

> The music will often have been chosen with an instinc-
> tive feel for what is suitable to the occasion. Whilst human
> love is the theme of many popular songs, the lyrics invari-
> ably contain references to eternal themes, such as the
> power of love to survive and overcome death. Denyer
> (1997, 199)

As Denyer identifies, many secular songs or pieces of music
have implicit theological, for example eschatological, themes
which reflect the hopes and desires of those who chose the
music as well as all who listen. In a recent BBC Radio 2 survey
of popular funeral songs the contribution of one listener read:

> 'Sloop John B,' The Beach Boys. As a believer in eternal
> life I find the lines 'I want to go home,' and 'this is the worst
> trip I've ever been on,' amusing and satisfying. 'I still haven't
> found what I'm looking for' by U2. I have a feeling that
> when the great day comes, I won't have! (Cowdrey 2006, 2)

Often in our postmodern era an eclectic mix of traditional
hymns and popular secular songs are included in the same
funeral. For example, one recent funeral which I shared in was
co-constructed with the sons of a man in his seventies, who

---

16 The song played regularly at Hibernian Football Club in Leith, Edinburgh
is often chosen to be played at the weddings and funerals of its supporters. 'Sunshine on Leith' by the Proclaimers (Reid and Reid 1988) is a moving song about
the ability of loving relationships to heal past hurts. Furthermore, it is a song of
thanksgiving which states that 'While the Chief, puts Sunshine on Leith,' those
present will give thanks to Him for his creation, especially the birth of the persons in the special relationship being marked or which has physically ended.

was not a church goer but in his latter weeks rediscovered anew something of the faith of his youth, included – 'Abide with Me' and 'The Lord's My Shepherd' as well as the song 'You Raise Me Up' by Brendan Graham (2001)[17]

> so I can stand on mountains
> You raise me up, to walk on stormy seas;
> I am strong, when I am on your shoulders;
> You raise me up . . . to more than I can be.

Classical music too connects us to eternal themes. For example, 'The Lark Ascending' by Vaughn Williams in its own way, like Graham's song, evokes images of resurrection. 'The possibility of eternity stirs in the hearts of every human being, and secular music, no less than sacred music, reflects this possibility' (Denyer 1997, 198).

Co-construction of, and sharing in, funerals enables:
The bereaved to regain some control in their situation.
In the immediacy prior to, and following, the death of a significant other there often is a desperate feeling of helplessness and loss of control for those grieving. There is nothing anyone can do to halt the dying process of the terminally ill, to bring the deceased back to life or to replay the moments before a fatal accident and have prevented it from happening. Parents interviewed after their babies death greatly appreciated the fact that they could make informed choices about rituals performed for their baby and, thus, regain some control over their circumstances. '*it [the funeral] does actually help you have this feel of kind of control . . . having something that you can influence in the situation where you are completely unable to influence events because it has been taken from you*' (Father 1).

---

17 A song which on one level may be taken to mean the influence of the deceased on family members to inspire them an individuals to be '[. . .]more than I can be'. Yet its lyrics also have meaning for the bereaved who have belief in a God who resurrects and gives hope in their grieving.

Co-construction enabled parents to have ritual ownership – to feel the ritual performed was their ritual for their baby. '*We could almost design our own funeral which is what we did, and everything we asked to be there was there, which was very pleasant*' (Mother 13). Hence, parents felt able to feel that they had invested something of themselves into the funerals they had helped to create. '*I think we did make it special*' (Mother 1). Parents appreciated being able to choose their level of involvement in: 1) co-construction – from writing their own funeral service to telling their story and then wanting the chaplain to create an appropriate ritual and 2) participation in the ritual itself– from reading a poem or prayer to bringing and laying down flowers. The content of ritual was teased out, negotiated and mutually agreed upon. '*We felt we wanted to say a few words but we never got pushed into doing anything we didn't want to do or, which was nice. He discussed our options as well. We all came to an agreement*' (Mother 7).

Co-construction also allowed bereaved parents to find a sense of meaning and purpose at a time when life felt devoid of such, by enabling them to do the best for their baby in circumstances which otherwise were beyond their control. Therefore, retrospectively, they could look back without regrets and feelings of unfinished business relating to how they had dealt with marking of their loved one's life and death, and disposal. This emphasises the importance of ritual leaders treating co-construction as a process rather than as an activity occurring during a single encounter: giving time for the funeral to evolve; to let it sit with the bereaved; to enable them to mull over it; to negotiate any adjustments with the ritual leader if they so wish and allow them to feel ownership and that they have truly done all that they can for their loved one.

I think between leaving the hospital and the funeral . . . the contact we had with the chaplain in between that time and then the actual funeral itself . . . if we had wanted to add anything into that a few days later then that would have been fine. We really just did it the best we could have done. And that was nice because we know there is nothing else that we could have done under the circumstances to make it any better than we had. (Mother 7)

An opportunity for the bereaved to tell, hear and reinterpret their story. Co-construction allowed parents to talk through or write out their experience and feelings, take stock, and for some, to reframe this part of their story. This helped them in their struggle to make sense of what had happened and in their attempt to put their experience into some sort of perspective. By listening to the chaplain's retelling and, thus, reinterpretation of the story of their baby's life and death during the funeral parents were able hear their experience of loss set in the framework of their wider family story and what significantly informed their particular narrative, including their beliefs and worldview. This enabled some parents to set their baby's death in some sort of context, which offered hope and comfort. *'It was to get some feeling of reassurance that it wasn't the end of the world I suppose even although it felt that way'* (Father 11).

Bosticcco and Thompson (2005, 4) sum up succinctly the role of storytelling and listening to those stories being retold within the process of ritualising the life and death of a loved one: 'stories contextualize events in terms of narrative structures with which people are already familiar'.

The bereaved to articulate their search for meaning.

All dying, deaths, and funerals have theological implications in the sense that they raise for all of us questions about 'the author and finisher of life'. (Streets 1996, 183)

Co-construction gives the bereaved an opportunity to verbalise their wrestling with issues of theodicy, their struggle to make sense of their experience of grief and their feelings in relation to the deceased when living and dead. Parents attempted to find some meaning in their experience of loss, within the framework of their belief system. '*Why did you give us gifts and take them away again*' (Father 6).

A church representative, within an established relationship of trust through non-judgemental listening may offer the bereaved permission to express questions of, and anger with, God and to articulate their doubts and feelings of abandonment.

> *I mean I have always had my religion, always have done but once that happened to me, what happened to us, you know, anybody would doubt their religion after that . . . . I don't know I just felt a bit more at ease (during and after the funeral) because it wasn't as if he was talking you know, you've got your religion, you've got to stick to your religion and these things happen, that wasn't who he was.* (Mother 7)

A ritual leader may utilise stories from her faith tradition in order to help normalise such depth of feeling and inner turmoil and, where appropriate, provide affirmation that mental and spiritual anguish is part of, not apart from, the journey of faith.

> How long, Lord, will you leave me forgotten?
> How long hide your face from me?
> How long must I suffer anguish in my soul,
> grief in my heart day after day?
>
> (Psalm 13: 1–2)

Expression of such torment not only has full biblical precedent but is also an important part of what the Hebrew mindset felt being human was about. After all, as Robert Davidson (1983, 10), former Professor of Old Testament at the University of Glasgow points out:

Some of these circumstances (out of which the psalms of lament emerge),[18] e.g. pain and death, are basic human experiences, others may be more culturally defined, but whatever the circumstances which give rise to them, it is noteworthy that psalms of personal lament occur with greater frequency in the Old Testament than any other type of psalm.

Affirmation of such questioning, searching and inner angst can also be given within the context of funerals by the utilisation of such texts as Psalm 13 or Jesus' cry of dereliction on the cross. Anger and accusations directed at God can be validated by reference to parts of Job's diatribe with his Maker. Davidson's (1983, 23) comments on the psalms of lament resonate with the best of pastoral care methodology:

> Many of the agonized 'whys' and 'how longs', which we find in the lament psalms, are witness to the fact that for many of the faithful in Israel life did not follow the script. In the face of this, the lament psalms seek to help the worshipper to live through the darkness of their experience. They make urgent appeal to God, but they do not claim either to understand or to explain the apparent irrationality of what has happened.

Ritual leaders, thus, have the opportunity during the process of ritualising a person's life and death to aid the expression and normalisation of many feelings and sentiments otherwise considered culturally inappropriate to publicly own and demonstrate in relation to their grief and understanding of God's place in it. This may be especially helpful for church members for whom having and articulating 'negative' feelings towards their Creator or questions about God's beneficence was previously a source of guilt and remorse.

---

18 The words in parentheses are mine and not Davidson's.

Even bereaved families who considered themselves non-religious found themselves doing theology when they were engaged in the process of co-constructing a funeral for their baby with a chaplain.[19]

> *[I]t's a complete contradiction because we have sat through all of this (the interview) and with the chaplain saying we are not overly religious and that's why we were a bit dubious about the chaplaincy because we weren't wanting a religious service then we've talked about angels and we've talked about touching with God.* (Father 13)

Together with a church representative, the bereaved may want to explore beliefs about the existence of an afterlife, critique the worship and ritual practice of the church (from the family's past experience), make observations about 'continuing bonds' and the communion of saints as well as wrestle with theodicy and lament the seeming absence of God in their situation. Such implicit theologising which naturally occurs out of the bereaved persons' experience, and their reflection on it, will greatly inform the content of the funeral – many of the bereaved's sentiments and phrases which arise out of their engagement with the church representative can be utilised in prayers, statements, blessings or words of committal by the ritual leader. However, it is important that the church representative is transparent about her intentions. She needs to make the family aware that this is fundamental to the process of co-construction, enabling the ritual to be grounded in the reality of their experience, theology and feelings and not an imposition

---

19 It is interesting to note that even though 13 out of 25 parents interviewed (12 couples were interviewed together and 1 mother on her own) said that they were not religious and had absolutely no affiliation to a local faith community only 1 out of the 13 funerals reflected on in the interviews did not mention God or some form of afterlife. This reflected the beliefs of the parents expressed during co-construction and not the chaplains.

of hers. At times the church representative may need to make the theologising more explicit and ask direct questions of the bereaved if they are hesitant or less forthcoming about their beliefs, especially regarding what they believe has happened to the essence of their loved one, in an eternal sense, now they are dead. This has to be done respectfully and gently so as not to appear like an inquisition or form of moral judgement or to cause further distress. Exploration with the bereaved of the lyrics of songs or hymns requested or their interpretation of, and meanings invested in, the music chosen can also help the church representative comprehend their beliefs more fully. If appropriately done within a relationship of trust such sensitive probing can help aid understanding of the survivors' eschato-logical hopes and fears, as well as of any other significant issues they may have in relation to the deceased.

The implication of such theologising and respect for the bereaved's (and where known the deceased's) beliefs means that not only will each funeral be unique in terms of the human stories told but also in terms of the way the divine story is interpreted and revealed.

> With this do-it-yourself attitude, people assemble their own personal belief system. One consequence of this personal-ization and individualization is the creation of a multiplicity of interpretation systems and eschatologies, and, likewise, ritual differentiation. (van Tongeren 2004, 137)

Affirmation of the bereaved. Chaplains affirmed parents, and their needs, as being important and worth responding to by engaging with their particular story and listening atten-tively and empathetically to them as part of the process of co-construction. '*He was a very good listener and he gave us time to say what we wanted to say . . . and it was actually really good*' (Mother 13).

For bereaved parents whose baby had died *in-utero*, having the opportunity to shape a funeral for their child helped to affirm their creative abilities at a time when they felt deep sorrow and guilt at having failed in their creation of a living and thriving child.

The bereaved to have some meaning and purpose in life in the immediacy of the death of a loved one. Being involved in a process of co-constructing and then sharing in a funeral for a loved one gives the bereaved a potential focus in life, quite literally something to live for, in the days following the death of a significant other.

> *It's hard to say what it would have been like without it (the funeral) but probably planning it was actually healthy. It was a good thing we had, in that time between the baby dying and the funeral, which was only sort of ten or twelve days. I think it was something that was almost positive for both of us, not positive, but it is in terms of what you are going through, rather than just the focussing on emptiness and nothing. When it (the death of their baby) happens, it is a big blank in front of you and your whole life is bleak and everything. It does actually give you something still to do for the baby.* (Mother 1)

Participation in funerals enables:
The bereaved to enact their feelings for, and relationship with, the deceased. Ritual enables the enactment of what is so difficult to put into words, at a time when language seemed lacking and limited. Funerals give families a context in which their deep feelings, needs, hopes and beliefs can be enacted. Moreover, actions and gestures, associated with, and carried out during ritual enable the bereaved to act out their relationship with the deceased and importantly contribute to feelings of ownership of the funeral. This has profound meaning and significance for the bereaved. '*It is also important to have the funeral, to make it your own – like choose the reading, and I chose to put some flowers on the coffin . . . and my husband carried the coffin*' (Mother 1).

You (to her husband) saying something was nice. . . . And I had a wee rose that I put on top (of her baby's coffin) which felt like the right thing to do. (Mother 8)

I suppose these kind of visual symbols. . . . It was comforting to us. (Father 8)

And also being able to touch . . . (Mother 8)

The coffin as well. (Father 8)

Some of these gestures of love and care were influenced by the bereaved's familial and cultural ritual inheritance.

I think from what I can remember its like going back to my gran when I took a cord (to help lower the coffin into the grave) for my gran like ten to twelve years ago and one of my older neighbours saying: 'You have to stay strong for your gran.' When I was taking this cord and lowering my gran and then just as soon as I had done it fine, great, come away and a single red rose to put in aaahhhh (tears). . . . That was it. (Father 5)

The desire for parents to act out their relationship with their dead baby was also informed by instinct and a deep need to take responsibility and parent their child as best they could, in the given circumstances. For some parents such ritual acts were perceived as their moral duty, an obligation that had to be fulfilled according to their understanding of what being a bereaved relative, in this case a parent, meant. Such gestures were performed with great dignity and required as much resolve as could be mustered at the time.

What if they (the funeral directors) had just taken the (baby's) coffin from the car and lowered it in would you have felt any different? (Mother 5)

Yes, probably yes. (Father 5)

What like you had missed out or . . . (Mother 5)

Yes, yes… (Father 5)

I should be doing that. (Mother 5)

Yes, well it's yours eh. Like if it was somebody else's wee child and you were in the background you'd be roaring and greeting. But there you find the strength to do it. You just find the strength. Oh no I wouldn't, I wouldn't want to do it any other way that way. . . . I wouldn't have wanted anybody else to do it. He's, he's my flesh and blood. I had to do it. Not anybody else. (Father 5)

But I wanted to walk with her. I carried her. . . . And I felt that like I could hold her, although she was in a box. I physically got a hold of her again. . . . Yes I wanted that to last as long as it could. You know its like don't rush this – this is important to happen here. . . . This is important but even although I still believe she's not there, it was still symbolic saying yes I will still take care. (Father 6)

The bereaved enact the significance of a funeral in many other culturally informed ways. For example, by the clothes they wear or encourage others to wear to their loved one's funeral. Within Western society, respect for the deceased and the significance of their death is still frequently marked by the gesture of wearing black. However, a steadily increasing trend in Britain is for the bereaved to wear bright clothes at the family's, or the deceased's, behest indicating that they don't wish the ritual to be a sombre affair. Moreover, such a gesture may be perceived as being symbolic of celebrating the deceased's life and/or their resurrection. Members of the deceased's family may buy new clothes specifically for the funeral or will wear clothes they knew that the deceased liked or had bought them; gestures of personal significance.

Ritual actions may help tell the particular story of the deceased and his/her relationships with those left behind as well as conveying more general sentiments such as love, care and respect. For example, an important part of the funeral of one patient who died in the hospice where I work involved his friends carrying his coffin into the crematorium over which were draped the strips of the two rival Glasgow football teams, Rangers and Celtic.[20] Following his retirement the deceased's day centred on conversations in his local pub, where he met with his friends, of the merits, or otherwise, of the soccer teams which they followed home and away. What was important to the life of the deceased, was enacted and symbolised at the start of his funeral; his relationship with his friends who along with him were united in their passion for football. Funerals are, therefore, occasions in which restrictive cultural norms may be transcended. They are, potentially, moments of creativity, where grace is glimpsed and love shared.

Following his death, the grandchildren of a well-loved grandfather, who were all aged 12 and below, responded to the suggestion that they might like to draw or paint something that for them encapsulated his character or their relationship with him. The deceased's widow felt it was an appropriate gesture for the paintings and drawings to then be used to decorate his coffin. Thus, as the coffin was carried into the crematorium the highly visible artwork was not only a reminder of the different facets of the deceased's life and personality but also symbolised the significance of the relationship between grandparent and his grandchildren.[21] Through their personal actions, the

---

20 The rivalry between these two teams is intense and historically is informed by religious and cultural differences – Celtic being a team traditionally linked with Roman Catholicism and working class Irish immigrants to the west coast of Scotland at the end of the nineteenth century and Rangers, a team steeped in Protestantism and having longstanding associations with the Orange Order. Affiliation to either of these teams is sometimes publicly expressed in the singing or chanting of sectarian songs by their supporters, especially when opposing fans are in the vicinity, occasionally spilling over into acts of violence.

21 When I saw the coffin decorated in such a way and observed all of the deceased's grandchildren proudly sitting in the crematorium I threw away my script for the beginning of the funeral. Instead, I felt it was important to articulate my response, which I sensed was shared by many present, to the creative actions of the children which encapsulated the love and regard they had for their grandfather and the place they had in his life. Doing so was a public acknowledgement and affirmation of the feelings and experience they had depicted as well as a means of further including them in what is culturally viewed as an adult ritual.

youngsters not only significantly contributed to the creation of a unique and personalised ritual but also helped enable the funeral truly to be owned by their family. Their actions, and the time, trouble and thought invested in them, was a fitting gift of love. The funeral became a means by which their deep feelings could be authentically and publicly expressed, acknowledged and validated.

Formerly, the most frequent way that many mourners enacted their response to the death of someone significant to them was to select and bring or send flowers to the funeral. This is no longer the case, as very often families choose to state in the newspaper death announcement that they wish only flowers from the immediate family to be displayed at the funeral. Increasingly, families invite those touched by the deceased's death to make a donation in lieu of flowers to an appropriate charitable organisation either by mail or as part of a retiring collection following the funeral. Contributing to such a body is an action which not only articulates the bereaved family's depth of feeling for the deceased but also enables survivors to do something practical in memory of the deceased and to counter their feelings of helplessness in face of the chief mourners' grief. It also supports the chief mourners' need to give back something to the institution where the deceased was cared for during their illness or to contribute to an organisation which seeks to prevent, alleviate or cure the means by which their loved one died. Those who contribute to such organisations may do so in part due to the stark reminder of their own mortality. They realise that they too may have need of, or benefit from, for example, the work of a local hospice, the Chest, Stroke and Heart Foundation or Cancer Research.

In concluding the discussion on ritual action, it is important to state that it is not just the language utilised in the ritualisation of an individual's life and death that cannot be forced upon the bereaved by the ritual leader; care must be taken to enable ritual acts (for use before, during and after the funeral) to also emerge from the process of co-construction.

Suffering to be transcended. Every parent interviewed described their child's funeral as a very emotional experience, whether the funeral was private or public. Paradoxically, however, many parents experienced something more or 'other' while sharing in the rite of passage. Ritual, therefore, was not only perceived by parents as an activity in which emotion was expressed and their relationship with their baby enacted but it also provided a context in which the extraordinary was experienced and grief transcended. *'I think it was a like a . . . little oasis of something'* (Mother 1). *'the kind of sense of peace in the place'* (Father 1). *'Well you said you found it uplifting'* (Mother 13 to her partner). *I am not really a spiritual man but . . . I just thought they were very good and kind words that he (the chaplain) said and very appropriate to what we were feeling at the time. It was quite . . . spiritual actually.* (Father 7)

Affirmation of the bereaved's beliefs. 'The service can direct us to the spiritual resources which can aid and encourage us' (Ainsworth-Smith and Speck 1999, 97–8). At a time of great distress, it was a relief and source of hope for parents that their beliefs, as well as their feelings and experience, were affirmed by the chaplain sharing in their funeral for their baby. An important part of meeting some parents' spiritual needs was that a person perceived to ensure ritual efficacy, that is a church representative, was involved in the funeral and in doing so articulated their eschatological aspirations. *'[T]o feel that he was sort of going somewhere to be with other people that loved him. I definitely felt a great comfort in that and just knowing that it had been done and he was accepted'* (Mother 7).

For some it was highly significant that biblical images were utilised to depict how their loved ones were cared for in the hereafter.

> *It was just quite calm and peaceful and made me think that they (her twins) had moved to a better place and that we would see them again – safe in God's arms or in the palm of*

his hands.[22] *I think that's how we felt . . . and that your mum (looking at her husband) was looking after them.* (Mother 11)

For others it was important that familiar words from their faith tradition (even when they were no longer active in the church) were shared during the funeral. For example, one couple chose the words of the Aaronic blessing to be said:

> May the Lord bless you and keep you;
> The Lord make his face to shine upon you,
> and be gracious unto you;
> May the Lord lift up his countenance upon
> you, and give you peace.
>
> (Numbers 6: 24–6)[23]

This blessing was chosen, as it is a statement of belonging – a blessing most commonly used during baptisms, a rite of passage when an individual is publicly acknowledged to belong, have a home, in the church in heaven and earth. The use of this blessing is symbolic of the parent's aspiration that their child has a place in a God's family where he belongs, is welcome and cared for and will be at peace; a place within the church which they regard as their spiritual home.

Ongoing ritual remembering. *'I had specifically chosen a burial so that I had somewhere to go back to'* (Mother 2). Over half of the parents interviewed spoke of returning to where their baby had been buried or cremated in the months following the funeral as a way of helping to maintain 'continuing bonds' with their child.[24] Pilgrimage to where their baby's funeral took place or where his body lies is indicative of a desire not to

---

22   Isaiah 49: 16.

23   From the Revised Standard Version of Scripture.

24   The interviews with parents took place 3 to 6 months following their child's funeral.

forget someone significant in their lives, someone who has an ongoing place in their family. *'We have got her burial place, our place of homage'* (Father 7). Such reverential visits which are often associated with the laying of flowers or tending of the grave are gestures which act out the relationship of the bereaved to the deceased, in this case ongoing parenting.

Mementoes from a funeral, for example, a printed order of service, the funeral eulogy or a poem or reading that was read, are often kept and read at moments of chosen significance to the bereaved. At a time in life when our senses are heightened, the funeral itself is associated with many memories for the bereaved. Bereaved parents could recall gestures made and performed during the funeral, the weather, the smell of the crematorium or of cut grass as they left the building, squirrels playing in the grounds, the music played or hymns sung and the clothes they chose to wear. Encountering such sights, smells and sounds again through chance or choice may cause the bereaved to remember not only their loved one's funeral but also what together they have shared and the influence of the deceased on their life.

Meeting Psychological Needs
Co-construction enables the bereaved to have markers to aid their decision-making

Chaplains not only explained the practicalities of ritual to parents, including the given parameters within which parents had to conform, but also shared the previous practices of other bereaved parents to act as benchmarks by which to gauge their own decision-making about possible options relating to ritual content. Moreover, the church representative shared resources, both sacred and secular, from which the bereaved might choose a reading(s), poem(s) or prayer(s) which reflected their story to be read during the funeral. Ritual leaders also commonly suggested a structure for each funeral, which other parents had found helpful, as a starting point to prompt discussion about ritual content. This was a great relief to parents and not only helped them to make informed choices but also enabled them to see a way forward in an unknown and confusing terrain.[25]

> *what normally happens? Because if it was completely free at that stage you would just be oooh . . . like too many decisions. I don't know . . . it really would be too much responsibility but within the sort of parameters, you know, it was almost like planning your wedding. There will be this sort of set of things you kind of have to do but you have variations between them, like music and stuff and I'd never thought.* (Mother 1)

> *He didn't make the decision for you, he gave you the options and you made the decision and he said well what about this and what about that.* (Mother 5)

Sharing in co-construction and funerals enables:

Regulation of grief.[26]   Church representatives heard during co-construction the parents' depth of grief and love for their baby and by relaying this publicly during ritual they validated and affirmed the bereaveds' feelings at a time when they not only felt vulnerable and fragile but also when they wondered whether their feelings were appropriate and culturally acceptable. Through retelling a family's story within the funeral context ritual leaders gave them permission to feel and be as they were. This enabled parents to feel that their particular response to the death of a loved one had been heard and taken seriously, understood and endorsed.

Co-construction also helped to sensitively regulate grief through the ritual leader offering a range of sacred and secular resources (which other bereaved persons had either found helpful or had written) that the recently bereaved utilised to aid expression of their spiritual turmoil and grief during the

---

25 Many parents were not just dealing with a baby funeral for the first time but having to a arrange a funeral for any loved one was a new experience.

26 A term utilised by Tony Walter in his book *On Bereavement: The Culture of Grief* (1999).

funeral, as well a sense of thanksgiving for the life of the deceased and the positive impact he had made on other's lives. It also helped the bereaved feel less isolated in their grieving – others had felt as they did. *'being given, lent, a book of readings was really comforting'* (Mother 1). Even if the bereaved do not choose to utilise such elegiac poems or prose in the funeral there is a sense of normalisation received from reading material which resonates with personal experience. Cole Jr. (2005, 205) empahsises such an effect in utilising what he terms 'melancholic elegy' whilst supporting those with complicated grief: 'affirmation (by reading the elegiac material) of one's profound loss is analogous to the sort of affirmation, or responsiveness, which feeds one's sense of self'.

Reality confrontation. Many parents found helping to create and then share in ritual marked the beginning of accepting the painful actuality of the death of their child. *'In a way you don't want to have the funeral because that's it, you know. It's an acceptance of what has happened'* (Mother 1). Accepting the reality of their loved one's death was described by some parents as a far from linear process. At times, their baby's death seemed all too real and at others as if the experience had never happened. For one father (12) his baby's funeral was paradoxically both at the same time.

> *It (the funeral) was really real but in my mind it was quite surreal. It was almost unbelievable that it was us, it was almost like watching something from a film that you are thinking God that's really bad but actually it was us which seemed almost unbelievable. It was us.*

One mother did not feel the reality of bereavement had hit her yet even as she was being interviewed over three months after her son's death. She, unlike her husband, chose not to visit her son's grave and in doing so consciously avoided seeking confrontation with the reality of his death. While it is perfectly normal for the reality of a loved one's death to take weeks to be

owned by the bereaved following their death, it is still imperative that any funeral service 'contains enough which says that
death is real' (Worsley 1994, 25). For the bereaved it is hard
enough to begin to face up to the death of a loved one without
the funeral only marking their life and not openly acknowledging their death.[27]

Funerals are a ritual when all who participate, no matter how
peripherally, are put in touch with their own mortality and the
fragility of human existence. It is not just the deceased's life
which is examined in the context of a crematorium or graveside setting nor is it just those who are closest to the deceased
that are reminded of their own impending death and that of
their loved ones.

> The funeral is a dramatic symbol of the fact that, despite all
> the advances of modern science, 100% of people still die. It
> gives us an opportunity to make real this simple fact and to
> respond emotionally and by our behaviour to the life and
> death of another person; it helps to initiate the process of
> grieving ; it reminds us that, both as individuals and as
> members of the social units to which they belong , people
> matter; it brings home the thought that we too are mortal
> and causes us to question a thousand habits of thought and
> behaviour which deny that fact. (Parkes 1990, viii)

Catharsis. 'There is a time for being alone with one's feelings – and a time for giving expression to them' (*The Guardian*
Editorial 2005, 30 reflecting on the role of public applause to
mark the significance to the football community in Britain of
the life and death of soccer maestro George Best). Parents felt

---

27 There is a danger of ritual leaders colluding with the bereaved to avoid making
    death explicit during a funeral and, thus, supposedly less painful for all con-
    cerned. If death is not made explicit both verbally and physically, by the visible
    presence of a coffin during a funeral, this may say as much about the church
    representative's wish to deny death as it does of the bereaved.

that they had cultural permission within the context of ritual to be themselves and express their feelings as they needed to at the time, without feeling awkward or uncomfortable. '*You are allowed to be upset and emotional*' (Mother 3). The cathartic experience of the funeral was found to be therapeutic. '*I thought the service had taken the anger away from me and made me be at peace*' (Father 9). The bereaved also found telling their story during co-construction or writing down some reflections to be read at the funeral similarly cathartic. '*Emotionally I would say it helped an awful lot. It gives you something to hang your grief on*' (Mother 3 commenting on writing something for her baby's funeral). Within the context of co-construction and the funeral itself, in both the ritualisation of grief as well as the enactment of it, a sensitive ritual leader may give the bereaved permission to disclose their inner selves and in doing so validate those feelings and their self-disclosing behaviour (Garrick 1994).

Funerals enabled:

Provision of milestones in the bereaved's journey of grief. A funeral helped to provide some orientation in parents' lives amidst the confusion in the days following their baby's death. Moreover, post-funeral rituals and other significant dates or appointments relating to their baby, for example follow up visits to the obstetrician or attending a memorial service, acted to provide parents with cairns to journey towards in the disorientating experience that is grief. '*(The funeral) Brought order to our lives again . . . we seemed to be just floating around aimlessly*' (Father 9).

A feeling of forward momentum in living with grief. Sharing in a funeral for their child enabled some parents to feel some sense of closure; an appropriate way of marking the end of their physical relationship with their baby — a time when parents literally had to physically let go of their dead babies. '*It was really for us to say goodbye — to have a clear ending*' (Mother 2). However, as part of such intimate leave-taking, funerals were also experienced as an opportunity for temporary reuniting of

111

parents with their baby, before the finality of physically letting go. Some felt that their baby's funeral significantly contributed to the feeling of the cessation of a period of acute grieving which dominated their lives. Thus, funerals were perceived as a watershed for many people in their experience of grief and facilitated a looking forward and moving on, though not forgetting. *'the funeral put one particular building block into the wall and let us move on to the next bit of grieving. It brought to a close a very, very bad chapter and I just wanted to move on from that bit'* (Father 12).

> For the essential meaning of the funeral is that in every ending there is a beginning. However we choose to conceive this idea, whether in terms of orthodox or unorthodox religious faith or even in angry protest that is another kind of faith, the funeral gives us hope. (Parkes 1990, viii)

Importantly, the funeral was also experienced as an ending to the period of limbo between the baby's birth and his burial or cremation, and, therefore, an end to parents' waiting for appropriate disposal. *'We were in limbo up till then. It was a way of bringing it to a natural end'* (Father 9).

Many parents described leave-taking from their deceased child not as a one-off event but as an ongoing process and that funerals were significant formal ritual moments in this process.

Meeting Social Needs

Participation in co-construction and in a funeral enables:

Recollection and creation of significant memories. In the sharing of memories during the process of co-construction the bereaved have the opportunity to tell their story and the story of the deceased, not just with a church representative but, of course, with family and friends. Telling and listening to stories is a social activity as well as a sacred one (Kelly 2007). Such a sharing of, and attentiveness to, stories not only enables a meaningful funeral to be performed but it is also ritual action in and of itself. The bereaved tell the stories of the deceased and their experience of grief to try to make sense of what has happened at a bewildering time: 'stories "impose a formal coherence on flowing soup"' (Weick 1995, 128 cited by Bosticco and Thompson 2005, 3).

Within the context of a funeral, such storytelling about different aspects of the deceased's life by the ritual leader, informed by the process of co-construction, and perhaps aided by a family member(s) and/or friend(s), help to create a rounded biography of the deceased. This enables those present to recollect their own particular memories and associations with the deceased and perhaps learn about hitherto unknown aspects of the deceased's life.

> To have a public, and accurate, biography told in the funeral may help mourners find an enduring place for the deceased in their lives – not least because the recounting of it there gives them permission to continue their own recounting in the weeks and months ahead. (Walter 1996, 22)

During a baby's funeral, the emphasis is less on sharing memories than in an adult funeral. However, there still will be some significant memories to recall even when a baby dies *in-utero*, for example, what the baby looked like or remembering how it felt to feel baby kick against her mother's abdominal wall, as well how it felt to be pregnant and the hopes and dreams the family shared for life with the baby. In baby funerals, the focus may well also be towards creating significant memories for the family rather than just helping them to recall those already formed. *'The memory that will stay with me for the rest of my life was carrying the wee white coffin into the crematorium. It is not an unpleasant memory. It is a good memory'* (Father 9). A funeral in and of itself , especially when co-created and owned by the deceased's family and involving family and friends, can create healing and positive lasting memories also. This may be of special significance if the bereaved felt particularly helpless during the deceased's fatal illness or there were unpleasant or upsetting memories around for them in relation to the time of death.

It is important also to note that a funeral for a person who dies before or during mid-life not only is about remembering and giving thanks for what has been it is also important to acknowledge the feelings of grief for what should have been; giving due attention to the dashed hopes and dreams for an expected shared future together.

Participation in a funeral enables:

Communal support to be given and received. Participating in a funeral is a social event. As Streets (1996, 182) puts it: 'funerals socialize the pain of dying and the grief of death for the living. It is an experience shared by the family, extended family, and community of the deceased'. *'Personally I've just taken a look behind me and just seen these people grieving and it's comforting. Just looking at people and just thinking you know they are there for you. They are there, here for you'* (Father 5 talking of his experience of his son's funeral).

> Weeping alone is painful. Grief is most powerfully eased when it can be shared. We look for a hand to hold, a shoulder to weep on, another body to cling to – anything that will reassure us that we are not alone, abandoned and helpless in the face of forces we do not understand. Death is the most powerful of these forces. (Carmichael 1991, 107)

There is a bond, both unifying and significant, felt by mourners present at a funeral when they are gathered to mark the life and death of someone they knew and who will continue to be part of their individual and collective memories.

At the funeral, an incidental community forms because of, and around, the deceased as an individual. The ritual collectivises those present; the concrete observance constitutes the congregation (the community) of that moment. (van Tongeren 2004, 139)

Such a bond may be further strengthened by the mourner's active participation in a shared ritual activity, for example, all standing as a mark of respect during the committal of the deceased into God's love and care or on the entry of the coffin into the church or crematorium.

> *We just wanted us, and close family, a nice little service mention-*
> *ing our baby, mentioning what he meant to me and my partner*
> *through the troubles we had been through and what he will*
> *always mean to us and also to my mum and dad, gran and*
> *granddad and aunts and uncles. . . . We chose a nice song to go in,*
> *my partner carried him in, and then the chaplain did her service.*
> *We chose to have flowers for him as well so everybody brought*
> *a posy of flowers, everybody that came, like grans, granddads,*
> *brothers, sisters.* (Mother 13)

Aldridge (2000, 195) refers to the 'social function of shared music' which aptly describes the hymn-singing at a funeral drawing together a possibly disparate group of people who are gathered to mark the life and death of someone they all knew and cared for yet many of those present may never have met each other before.

> Hymn-singing is a communal activity and with everyone standing up to sing the hymn as one body. Even if some are holding their hymn books before expressionless eyes and motionless lips, there is solidarity in the action. 'The Lord's my Shepherd' and 'Guide me, O Thou great Redeemer' sung shoulder to shoulder become anthems of common humanity and a shared mortality. (Deyner 1997, 200)

Moreover, listening together to a favourite piece of music or song of the deceased facilitates collective and individual ritual remembering – the music enables a union of purpose.

> A person who has died is no longer buried from the local Christian community, but from an incidentlly composed congregation of friends and relatives. Because of this, a funeral also takes on the character of a reunion. (van Tongeren 2004, 139)

In addition, the refreshments or wake following the funeral also may have the atmosphere of a reunion, where instead of recalling stories centred on experiences at school or university, reminiscing is focussed on life shared with the deceased between a dispersed and fragmented group of friends and family.

Public communication of the bereaved's changes in social status and depth of loss. Funerals help to acknowledge changes formally in the social status of the bereaved. It is during a funeral that a wife whose husband has just died publicly takes on the role of a widow and a parent whose baby has died is recognised not only as bereaved but also as a bereaved parent. 'Society may need rites of passage to realign and clarify the interactions between people in different stages and conditions' Ramshaw (1987, 41). Through the articulation of their baby's story and their experience of grief by the ritual leader as well as by their enactment of their relationship with their child in a formal ritual context, those in their wider family and circle of friends were able to understand better what they were living through. van Tongeren (2004, 137) writes about an allied perception in relation to adult funerals:

> The last thing which they (the bereaved) can do for their loved one is to provide a good, beautiful funeral. In this, they can at the same time give shape to their own grief and emotions. By doing justice to the personality of the

deceased through the liturgy, the loss of those who remain behind is also indirectly dealt with. It allows all to understand what the surviving family must miss and, as it were, justifies their grief.

Meeting Practical Needs
Co-construction enables clarity regarding the practical arrangements for a funeral

Parents were anxious about the basic practicalities relating to what happened during the funeral. *'Like you know, almost well talk me through it minute by minute as I do not know. Are we going to sit down or what happens'* (Mother 1). Co-construction allowed the chaplain and parents to talk through the practicalities involved in ritual and ensured the bereaved were aware what each ritual entailed. The ritual leader was also able to give the bereaved information about what needed to be done and who normally did what in relation to the organisation of a baby's funeral. Information about these practical aspects of funerals greatly reduced parental anxiety. *'We were really well prepared for when we were going up there (the cemetery) and it was nice because it took a lot of the stress out of it'* (Mother 7).

> *For families that's a traumatic time thinking I have got to organise this funeral now for this baby and the chaplain took a lot of the stress and strain from us. I mean dealing with a lot of that and giving us guidance by saying you know this has got to be done but we (the hospital) will take care of that.* (Father 13)

6

Ritual Leaders: The Need for Integrity of Theology and Practice

Do You Find It Hard Not to Mention the Lord?

This chapter involves theological reflection on the practice of co-constructing and sharing in funerals with church members and with those who would call themselves non-religious. Its content was stimulated by the above question being put to me by a funeral director as we stood at the door of an Edinburgh crematorium. I had been participating, along with family members and friends, in the explicitly non-religious funeral of a woman who had died in the hospice where I work. My role had primarily been to help the family come to some agreement about the content and structure of the funeral (informed by my theology, experience and knowledge of bereavement theory), share some of the thinking behind this and to act as master of ceremonies during the ritual. Neither I nor any of the other participants mentioned God, possibilities of an afterlife or any other religious belief or affiliation. Yet, being part of this ritual marking of a unique human life through song, music, words, silence, visual art, ritual action and touch had been a profoundly moving and uplifting spiritual experience. This did not just reflect what was said, sung or done but how these actions were performed. None present had been passive observers; all had been active participants. For me, the Lord was implicitly a large part of not only the funeral but also that which had informed its mode of construction. Not only did the presence and involvement of a church representative embody the presence of Christ during the ritual but also a theological outworking of Christ's life and teaching underpinned the approach taken to collaborative authorship of the funeral and the manner of its shared performance.

Ritual Leaders Owning and Utilising the Paradox of Power and Risk

In order for Church representatives to be able to create and share in meaningful funerals with the bereaved it is clear from reflecting on the experience of bereaved parents, a balance between the appropriate use of authority and vulnerability is required.

During the Co-construction of Funerals
Church representatives have ritual authority

The principal reason why bereaved parents approached chaplains to help them with the ritual marking of the life and death of their baby was that they considered a church representative to be culturally the most appropriate person to perform their child's funeral, irrespective of whether they were a member of a community of faith or not.

> *I was brought up to think that to officiate something like that you needed someone, well sort of in authority ... I felt it would not have been done right if one of us got up and conducted the service. You know sort of read the eulogy even though we had done it ourselves. . . . You need someone, either a minister or someone like that to do it completely.* (Father 3)

Moreover, chaplains were perceived to have the appropriate training, competence and experience to perform rituals. In asking a church representative to help construct and perform a loved one's funeral, many bereaved people feel in doing so they are doing the best they can for the deceased.

> *The chaplain has had training in proper public speaking ... so even though you've written the words, you know what's coming it*

*is still different you know. Especially spoken properly . . .
I suppose it is like the difference between reading poetry and
hearing someone else read it.* (Mother 3)

Western society still associates a chaplain or clergyperson's
role with ritual. This is part of our perceived priestly function –
not only can church representatives say the right words but
they are also entrusted with being able to do the right thing,
the right way. Following the death of a significant other when
life seems disordered and directionless people within and out
with local communities of faith still commonly look to church
leaders to perform ritual marking. Ramshaw (1987, 57) puts
it well:

> At times when people need a sense of order or meaning, a
> handle on ambivalence or an approach to mystery, it may
> be the ritual authority of the pastor that draws them, even
> if they do not consciously define their need as having any
> ritual dimension.

Chaplains were perceived to fulfil primarily two different
roles during the process of co-construction. The role they performed at any one time depended upon parents' needs at
specific moments in their grief. Both roles involved listening,
thus, enabling chaplains to weave parents' particular stories into
funerals but each had their distinctive qualities.

Church representatives act as an unhurried supportive presence
In the immediacy of their grief parents experienced chaplains
as individuals who were prepared to be with them and offer
them their time and a supportive presence. *'It was someone to
lean on . . . someone that understood'* (Father 7). Parents appreciated that, in contrast to other caring professionals and visitors,
church representatives initially listened rather than trying to
offer advice or care physically for them. *'Listening rather than
trying to help, trying to tell you this. Her approach was so different to*

everybody else who was like – this is what has happened, this what is going to happen . . .' (Mother 1).

Such a presence in times of great distress makes a great impression as Lawbaugh (2005, 27) states:

> As we look back on those who have given us the greatest comfort or those who have had the most powerful impact upon our lives (such as family members, teachers and best friends), we not remember them so much for what they said rather than for who they were. We remember them mainly for their ministry of presence, not their words.

Being present with another in their grief not only means a church representative has to make herself available to the bereaved but it also means risking exposure to grief, pain and questions to which there are no easy or ready-made answers. In other words, to create meaningful funerals which help to facilitate the grieving of the bereaved ritual leaders have first to risk being human alongside them. The feelings, experience and search for meaning of the bereaved has to be heard and understood before their story and relationship with the deceased can be reinterpreted and re-enacted during the funeral. Bruce Rumbold (1986, 39), an Australian hospital chaplain and pastoral theologian puts it this way:

> A helping relationship helps by the helper making himself vulnerable – running the risk not just of professional inadequacy but of personal helplessness in order that change may come about. If the helper is not open to change, neither will the patient be open.

Former chaplaincy colleagues Ian Ainsworth-Smith and Peter Speck (1999) helpfully describe ways in which church representatives, especially clergy, may avoid subjecting themselves to the depths of grief. First, because we might feel (and possibly others) we are set apart with special insights and access to higher truths and, thus, an assumption is made that we already know how people are feeling and what they are living through. Avoidance here is failure to engage with the bereaved's actual experience and in offering glib absolutes, biblical or otherwise, when survivors struggle to make sense of their loss. Second, as ministers we may hide behind our clerical attire or theological jargon as a means of maintaining power and authority within a caring relationship where vulnerability, not posturing, and silence not meaningless words are required. Third, prayer or formalised ritual can be used as a means of escape from emotion rather than potentially facilitating (and affirming) the expression of feelings and deepening honest communication (including wrestling) with God. Fourth, a church representative giving the impression of real or imagined busyness conveys to the bereaved that she has neither the time nor the inclination to engage with their pain.

'So the Word became flesh; he made his home among us' (John 1: 14). God, in Jesus, actively chose to make Godself vulnerable, to live through the whole range of human experiences including the joy of weddings, the intimacy of human relationships, the distress of bereavement and even death itself. On seeing Martha, whose brother Lazarus had died, and her friends weeping because of their loss, Jesus also wept (John 11: 35).

In dealing with the distress of the bereaved, the task of the church representative is not just to listen. It is also to wait, to wait with the bereaved until they are ready to take the step towards working with the ritual leader to co-author their loved one's funeral.

> By remaining *with* people, but at the same time refusing to take the escape from pain they seek, we can restore their courage to voice their deepest fears and express the anguish which they find threatening. Our main task is to wait and watch with them, that simple service which Jesus asked for (in vain) from his friends. (Campbell 1981, 44)

Church representatives act as interpretative guides

Parents, once their minds turned to planning funerals for their baby, found that co-construction was an empowering experience facilitated by a church representative who was perceived to be discerning as to how involved parents wanted to be in the process. *'He obviously gauged that we were emotionally strong enough and able enough to do something for ourselves. I could imagine it would not be the right thing for everyone'* (Mother 3).

Chaplains did not dominate construction of rituals but neither did they leave parents to make decisions unsupported or without guidance or information about cultural norms. *'The chaplain's suggestions actually brought out what we wanted'* (Mother 9).

Chaplains acted as guides, as well as companions, along parents' journeys of grief as they sought to do the best for their deceased loved one in co-creating an appropriate funeral and deal with their grief in a manner appropriate for them. Church representatives were felt not just to offer general guidance but also to listen to parents' particular stories, to interpret them within the context of her experience, training and worldview, and to respond appropriately.

In A. A. Milne's (1928) *Winnie the Pooh,* one of the many adventures the very fallible, and hence, likeable Pooh embarks on is to go hunting for a Woozle in the dark Forest, accompanied by his friend Piglet. Ernest Shepherd, who illustrated Milne's work, beautifully depicts the two brave sojourners walking into the unknown, unsure of what lies ahead and how they might deal with it. It is Pooh's search, he leads the way, and his companion, also frightened and rather uncertain, walks beside him. Pooh sets the pace, the direction and tone for their search and Piglet travels with him. Parents in this study appreciated chaplains being an unhurried supportive presence, someone willing to accompany them into the unknown, immediately following their baby's death – to share their anxiety, fear and be with them in their disorientation. They appreciated that the church representative did not try to direct their search for meaning, hasten their decision-making, cut short their storytelling or suppress their expression of emotion. However, like Pooh, there came a time when parents wanted to find a way forward, and an end to incessant confusion – going round in circles, retracing the same footsteps in their journey of grief. In Pooh's seeking, it is Christopher Robin, who, from up a tree, sees the bigger picture of Pooh's journey and offers his insight (that Pooh in fact had been going round and round following his own footsteps in the snow not that of an ever-increasing number of Woozles) and information as to how to find a possible way forward out of the dark Forest. This enables Pooh to pause and reflect on his experience and the information given to him, then in his own time make the decision for himself to take a particular path. Moreover, the gentle way in which Christopher Robin shares his knowledge and understanding prevents Pooh from feeling ridiculous and judged but rather to feel affirmed and loved.

Although the bereaved do need the companionship of those who are willing to accompany them along their particular journey of grief, they also require someone to help guide them through such desolate and disorientating times offering signposts and markers for decision-making along the way. With respect to enabling the bereaved to co-construct a meaningful funeral for their deceased loved one, ritual leaders may share with them information regarding practicalities and content so they can regain some control and make informed decisions. Thus, the relationship between a church representative and a bereaved individual or family is never equal. There is a degree of mutuality in a caring relationship – both church representative and the bereaved are human beings who may learn from, or be changed by their encounter(s) with, one another. However, it is an 'asymmetric mutuality' (Rumbold 1986, 39). Irene Bloomfield (1978, 13 cited by Foskett and Lyall 1988, 103), a psychotherapist, helpfully comments:

If there is an expectation of total mutuality, the relationship is one of friends and neighbours, but is precisely
because friends and neighbours have not been able to give
what was needed that people feel the need to consult a
professional.

Moreover, there is a 'mutuality of need' (Campbell 1981,
100) within any relationship which a potential carer needs
to be aware of when seeking to support another. The church
representative as well as the bereaved bring needs to their relationship, which at least in part, may be met for the ritual leader
by her involvement.

In the relationship established between church representative
and the bereaved, the bereft individual or family look to the
ritual leader for guidance, information and a sharing of her
previous experience to help them shape a relevant funeral for
them and their loved one. It is important that during such a
relationship that church representatives acknowledge the power
they have and not pretend that they are in a relationship of
equals. In utilising their authority in a discerning and sensitive
way not only is their relationship with the bereaved enhanced
but the funeral they co-construct together will be all the more
personalised and meaningful.

Church representatives act as facilitators of theologising
As a bereaved family share its struggles and search to find meaning in their experience of loss during the process of
co-authoring a relevant funeral with a ritual leader together
they are doing theology. This is not at the church representative's behest but is a need of the bereaved – to be given
permission, time and space to externalise difficult questions of
unjust suffering, of the possibility of the existence of a God, let
alone a beneficent or non-malevolent one, and possibilities
an afterlife. The role of the ritual leader is to facilitate such
an exploration when such a need is discerned and where

appropriate offer the stories from her tradition as a means of affirming and validating their wrestling.[1] The bereaved are not looking for answers from a church representative in their acute grief but an opportunity to give vent to what is a deep and heartfelt desire to try to make sense of what has happened and why. Not uncommonly, there may be a need for the bereaved to be angry with God, perhaps directed at God's perceived representative, or to apportion blame to a God that should have intervened or come to the aid of the deceased.

In enabling the bereaved to participate in such theological exploration and expression church representatives are following in the wake of other theologies and theologians who have encouraged the marginalised and the vulnerable to articulate their struggles to understand God's relationship with them and the world (in this case dominated by loss) they inhabit.[2] During the process of co-construction, church representatives are doing theology in dialogue with the bereaved. Dorothy Solle (1997, 26–7, cited by Foskett [1999, 125]) emphasises the importance of theology being informed by the powerless:

> a right theology needs people in the middle to communicate and ask questions, in other words complaining women, widows and other uneducated people. I don't want to do any more theology without listening to the interlocutors, or being clear who they are.

---

1 Here again the psalms of lament, the story of Job's wrestling with God in regard to his misfortune and Jesus' words of dereliction from the cross may be utilised with sensitivity as examples of a human response to dying and death and loss and desolation, even from those who we perceive are close to God and from a source that many understand is more about faithfulness than doubts, answers rather than questions and acceptance rather than rage.

2 John Foskett (1999, 124–5) provides a helpful reminder of pastoral theologians who have enabled the marginalised in Western society to have a voice – 'Reit Bonn-Storm (1996) for women, Archie Smith (1982) for black people, Nancy Eisland (1994) for the disabled, and Stephen Pattison (1994) for those with mental health problems […].'

*Church representatives handing over ownership of funerals
to the bereaved*

It is not just theologising that the church in the form of its representatives has traditionally monopolised; the church has likewise historically controlled the content of funeral liturgies. According to bereaved parents interviewed a key requirement which challenges a church representative to risk much to create meaningful funerals is for the church, in the form of ritual leader, to hand over the ownership and control of the funeral content to the bereaved, if they want it. The church representative enables this to happen by sharing resources, practical information and a possible order for the funeral, thus, aiding the bereaved to make informed choices – making the funeral theirs for their deceased loved one. A ritual leader may offer guidance from her experience and knowledge but what is suggested may not be what a particular family wants. Ultimately, if they do not concur and negotiation proves fruitless the bereaved have the choice to approach another ritual leader, Christian or otherwise. Entering into a relationship with the bereaved where funerals are co-authored does mean being open and vulnerable but it does not mean that anything goes. Risk for church representatives is not just about letting go of control it is also about being honest in relation to sharing possible implications of certain choices made and expressing personal needs, boundaries and theology. Risk is, therefore, also about holding onto personal and theological integrity and may mean dealing with displeasure, unpopularity or even rejection.

Ritual Leaders Utilising Power and Authority
During funerals church representatives have a priestly role, including acting as:

Conduits to the divine. Such authority was also linked with ritual efficacy – the idea that the prayers and petitions of a person in a leadership role in the church would be more effective than the interviewed parents' own or anyone else's.

Involving a chaplain in their baby's funeral provided more assurance for parents as to the eternal destiny of their deceased loved one; the church representative acting as a mediator between a child's earthly parents and the Divine Parent.

> '*They are in touch. . .*' (Father 13)
> '*With God and things so you associate the chaplaincy with that and that's why a prayer from a chaplain means more than from just an ordinary person.*' (Mother 13)
> '*She opened the door for him (baby) to go into God's house . . . she could show him the right path.*' (Mother 9)

Event co-ordinators. Whether parents had religious beliefs or not, the chaplain working with them was understood as the person who held the funeral together, acting as the glue or link which made its different components one. Therefore, if others were participating in ritual action or singing or speaking during the funeral it was the church representative who co-ordinated such involvement. No matter who was actively involved in participating in ritual marking and how, parents perceived the need of someone who could be trusted: '*to be there and take control*' (Father 5).

Creators and managers of sacred space.[3] Ritual leaders not only controlled what happened within the context of funerals they were also perceived to create the contextual boundaries of the ritual in terms of time and space. '*If you imagine him with long arms and just keeping everyone round the graveside. . . . he just held everybody together*' (Mother 5). Church representatives, thus, take on a protective parental role during a funeral,

---

3   The space itself becomes sacred due to the 'intention' (Davies 1994) of those who enter or are present in it. In this case mourners, informed by cultural norms and past experience, come seeking and expecting a time in which they can be themselves and express themselves as they need to, individually and corporately, for those few minutes in their journey of grief.

corporately holding and sustaining mourners as one body at a time of great distress – the bereaved taking comfort from being held in such a sanctuary with others who are similarly vulnerable. Humans for generations, in times of emotional fragility have sought such safe havens in the storms of life created by a trustworthy and caring Parental Figure – 'how precious is your unfailing love. Gods and frail mortals seek refuge under the shadow of your wings' (Psalm 36: 7).

'A funeral is an occasion where change takes place; it must be located in a safe place where people can let go, and come out reconstructed' (Durston 1990, cited by Walter 1990, 124). The church representative is the one who co-ordinates the formation of a safe environment – marking the boundaries, the beginning and end of funeral – within which people can feel secure enough to allow often conflicting feelings, inner wrestling and searching to be acknowledged and perhaps expressed, both individually and collectively. Carr (1985, 116) describes mourners being in a state of 'managed regression' controlled by the ritual leader within the context of funerals. The bereaved are in a state of bewilderment and disorientation, yet are seeking to comprehend their experience of loss and put the story of their loved one and their relationship with deceased into some sort of context. The church representative, a parental authority figure, facilitates the mourners' engagement with death, the story of the deceased, their family and community stories and, where appropriate, the divine story within a time and space purposefully created to permit the bereaved to be vulnerable and let their feelings surface. During funerals, the depths of the human psyche and soul may be touched and that which otherwise remains hidden or denied may be faced and named, and the desire to deal with what is discovered may be found. It is the responsibility of the ritual leader to help shape and maintain a structure which enables the bereaved to do so without being overwhelmed or destroyed and to hold the participants during their state of transition and potential transformation. Thus, the church representative provides for the survivors' 'confirmation, protection and sustenance' (Green 1987, 87) and in doing manages a space in which grace may be experienced and healing may begin.

> *After that one (baby's funeral) you could actually feel as if someone had got hold of your shoulders or whatever and just pulled . . . em . . . I felt as if a big weigh had been taken off. . . . It was just weird. It was as I mentioned, I said that to my wife as well, I think it was about the first, the only funeral that I have actually felt that – to that extent anyway . . . yeah . . . very therapeutic.* (Father 3)

Professional wordsmiths.[4]

> We're going to need the minister
> to help this heavy body into the ground.
>
> But he won't dig the hole;
> others who are stronger and weaker will
> have to do that.
> And he won't wipe his nose and his eyes;
> others who are weaker and stronger will
> have to do that.
> And he won't bake the cakes or take
> care of the kids . . .
>
> No, we'll get the minister to come
> And take care of the words.
> (From *The Minister* by Anne Stevenson
> 2003, 57)

Stevenson's poem sums up parents' perceptions in this study, of the chaplain's role as a wordsmith who had sufficient

---

4   The term wordsmith was used in a previous publication utilising the experiences of bereaved parents to inform the practice of hospital chaplains working in obstetric and neonatal units (Kelly 2007, 204).

experience, expertise and training to be able to articulate what needed to be said for their sake and the sake of the deceased within an emotionally charged context. Church representatives were perceived as verbalising how parents felt about their baby, their loss, their hopes for his future care and ongoing place in their family. For those parents with Christian beliefs, deeply held or questioned, the chaplain's verbal assurance of the baby's eternal destiny, of God's involvement in their distress and God's love and care for them, as well as their baby, was significant. *'For me anyway he was there as I say the conduit to God but also as a man saying* our *words. . . . He was just there as a mouthpiece really'* (Mother 3). During the funeral, the ritual leader was seen as a storyteller; telling the story of the deceased, and in the process reinterpreting that story, in relation to their family, the wider human, and where appropriate, the divine story.

Embodiment and enactment of the divine story. To what extent a church representative proclaims God's story within a funeral and offers the bereaved the opportunity to reinterpret the deceased's story in light of the Christian meta-narrative depends on the beliefs and needs of the bereaved and the response of the ritual leader to them. However, irrespective of the extent to which the Divine story is articulated for some parents it was embodied by the church representative. 'The presence of a chaplain or "holy person" helps "bless" the event with his symbolic presence' Ramshaw (1987, 71).

Chaplains were understood as representing God's presence with the bereaved in their grief and pain. They were also perceived as a representative of the church – the community of faith on earth and in heaven to which parents felt they belonged (whether they were active members or had historical connections). Moreover, chaplains symbolised hope and resurrection in this life, for parents, and in the next, for their babies. *'To me he (the chaplain) represented where my boy was going'* (Mother 5).

Furthermore, the divine story is enacted by the church representative during the funeral, incarnating God's relationship with the bereaved and the deceased. The significance of the shaking or holding of a hand, a hug or the putting of an arm round a shoulder when the bereaved may be very distressed, for example, as they enter the crematorium or settle in their seats before the funeral commences cannot be underestimated. One mother described how at the beginning of her son's funeral the chaplain escorted her to her seat and sat with her as her husband carried his coffin into the crematorium.

> *She was very kind and when we walked into the crematorium, into the chapel, my husband stayed back to carry the coffin and the chaplain actually walked me down and sat with me in the pew at the front until my husband had walked up and placed the coffin. She then moved on to give the service. I wasn't ever left alone to sit there by myself, she did sit with me and ... em ... that was very comforting of her because it would be very daunting just to sit there yourself.* (Mother 9)

The ritual leader ensuring the deceased is treated with respect and dignity during the funeral is significant. For example, coming out from behind a lectern or down from any pulpit and turning, facing and addressing the deceased when blessing or committing him into God's care in the hereafter. By such actions, a church representative conveys that the deceased matters as an individual not just to her and to the mourners who are gathered but also to God.

Acknowledgement and Use of Power and Authority

Sam Wells, an Anglican priest and Christian ethicist, reflects in *Power and Passion* (2007) on the power minor characters involved in Christ's Passion had in their context and on the power we have as human beings, however ordinary we feel we are, in the choices we make and the roles that we perform in our own particular situations. In doing so, Wells (2007, 16) comments insightfully: 'People seldom acknowledge their power but find it easier to articulate their passion.' Supporting the bereaved requires passion – a passion to care for those bruised and bewildered by their experience of loss and a passion to embody the love of Christ in a way that is meaningful for both bereaved and carer. However, to sensitively help meet the spiritual, psychological, social and practical needs of those who grieve, church representatives not only need to be passionate but also require to have some insight into, and ownership of, the authority and power invested in them by the bereaved. In utilising power with discernment and choosing to be vulnerable when appropriate, church representatives embody a model of ministry enacted by Jesus. In this sense, ritual leaders are required to use their power in a way that enables them to help and empower the bereaved rather than control and dominate. Jesus attracted the marginalised, weak and vulnerable in society. He was sought out because he was perceived to have power and authority in his teaching, healing and defiance of what he considered unjust. However, in his relationships with the isolated and powerless Jesus did not seek to manipulate or subjugate. He sought to meet the spiritual, psychological, social and physical needs of those who came to him through empowerment and allowing them to make informed choices in response to his storytelling and actions. Cooper-White (2004, 59) talks of the appropriate use of power in caring relationships as lived out by Jesus:

> the authority conferred on the helper exists not because of any intrinsic superiority, but because of a disproportionate fiduciary (that is, entrusted) responsibility for the welfare of the other. In this sense, there is power in the helping role, but when it is exercised faithfully, it is exercised in the sense of power-for rather than power-over.

Frances Ward (2005, 169), an Anglican priest and pastoral theologian, postulates that there are different forms of power in a student–supervisor relationship. Her use of Hawkins and Shohet's (2002, 94) categorisation of three types of power in such a relationship has relevance for deepening our understanding of the different aspects of authority church representatives might possess when seeking to co-construct and share funerals with the bereaved. First, *role power* which is inherent in the supervisor's (or in this case the ritual leader's) role. This aspect of power is utilised, for example, in creating and managing the sacred space within which a funeral is performed. It is important that a ritual leader has the self-assurance to utilise this type of power with a degree of conviction if those sharing in the funeral are going to be able to feel safe and secure enough to express themselves as they need to within the ritual context. Sawchuk et al. (2007, 499), in an exploration of the power clergy have in relation to members of their congregation, comments helpfully:

> Of importance . . . is the assertion that a great deal of power is derived from the professional role itself. This stance is related to the trust generally placed in the clergy as respected authority figures; power is also a function of the great responsibility that pastors have for their con-gregants (and others whom they share rituals with).[5]

Second, *personal power* which is the authority any individual supervisor (or ritual leader) is understood to have due to the student's (the bereaved's) perception of their 'expertise and experience' (Ward 2005, 169). Bereaved parents saw chaplains as having the necessary training, experience and wherewithal to be the appropriate person to help conduct their babies' funerals. Third, *cultural power* whose source is the dominant social and cultural group which a supervisor (or ritual leader) could belong to.

> In northern Europe a person with cultural power would be someone who was born within the white, western majority group. This power is emphasized if that person is

---

5 The words in parentheses are mine and not Sawchuks.

male, middle class, heterosexual and able-bodied. (Hawkins and Shohet 2002, 95)

Such a description of those persons with cultural power describes the majority of church representatives who would be relating to the bereaved with a view to co-authoring and sharing funerals with them in the Western world. Hence, it is of significance that ritual leaders are aware of this given aspect of power and how it may affect the manner in which they relate to the bereaved and to what extent the bereaved are able to share of themselves with a church representative. This especially may be the case if the bereaved are not familiar with Christian culture and feel embarrassed and disadvantaged in the company of a clergyperson who makes it obvious he most definitely is! Each of us is nested in particular cultural groups and a high degree of reflexivity is required to prevent the cultural power ritual leaders frequently possess to subordinate others in caring relationships.

Vulnerability When Sharing a Funeral
Significance of ritual leader's performance

Paradoxically, though some parents perceived the church representative as incarnating a story which symbolised transcendence and power, the manner in which the ritual leader embodied the divine story was a reminder of the immanence of God – a loving God who shares our human suffering, is open to our pain and moved by it. For many parents, the manner in which rituals were performed and how words were spoken was as important as the choice of words used. Chaplains were observed to be touched and moved by their involvement and felt to speak with genuine feeling. *'An awful lot of emotion (during the funeral), an awful, awful lot of emotion'* (Father 5). *'Yes, oh yes. You could feel it . . . from everybody, even the chaplain. You just got that sort of vibe'* (Mother 5). It was, therefore, highly significant for the bereaved that the ritual leader was perceived to be sharing in a ritual with them not doing the funeral for or to them. The church representative was experienced as empathetic and actively responsive to their feelings not just during the construction of the funeral but also during the ritual itself. However, it was equally important for mourners that while the church representative made herself available to the present moment in an emotional context she also remained detached and professional enough to perform her role as event co-ordinator and manager of the sacred space as part of her priestly function.

Parents also felt that chaplains believed what they said. The church representatives were perceived to give of themselves when sharing in ritual – they were committed to, and caught up in the ritual moment, and performed the ritual to the best of their ability. *'she really did give a beautiful lovely service. Em, there was so much feeling in it'* (Father 13). Chaplains were also felt to perform funerals with real sensitivity and compassion – responding appropriately to the emotional fragility of families within the context of funeral rituals. *'He performed the funeral in a very gentle way'* (Mother 2). How the funeral was performed was as important as its content.

Furthermore, it was significant for parents that chaplains did not rush or hurry through funerals. The church representatives involved were perceived to allow parents to have time during and after rituals to attend to and express their feelings when they needed to. Ritual leaders conveyed the significance of the baby and the parents' experience of loss partially by the unhurried nature of their performance.

Ritual leader as sustainers of grief

Paradoxically, church representatives sharing in funerals not only have an important role in maintaining control of the structure, boundaries and flow of the ritual but they also have a critical function in allowing grief to be and be expressed. Ritual leaders are representatives of a tradition which historically has allowed and encouraged grief, sorrow and desolation to be acknowledged and uttered, privately and publicly, personally and corporately. However, inheritors and preservers of this tradition have struggled to remain faithful to such lamentation.[6] Chaplains were felt by bereaved parents to be sustainers of grief, acknowledging its reality, ambiguities and confusing nature, which was tangibly palpable during funerals. By naming grief and allowing it to be openly present, ritual leaders prevented its denial or avoidance by those present. In doing so, a church representative is not controlling or manipulating pain or sorrow nor keeping it at arms length. *'On one hand she was trying to be with us, dealing with all this grief, and on the other, not controlling but orchestrating events'* (Mother 1). In taking such a role, a church representative exposes herself during a funeral, as well as in its co-construction, to grief. However, this does not necessarily mean that she is always comfortable with it. The bereaved appreciated how difficult that it may be for ritual leaders to allow grief and its expression to be while also enacting various priestly roles during their child's funeral.

> *he's just got this wee posse of people that, he's in control of and that's just like taking people and holding them all in. Eh . . . I mean what can he be feeling inside . . .? He's got strength to stand and do that as well.* (Father 5)

If the church representative is able to stay with the emotion expressed by the bereaved individually during co-construction and corporately during the funeral, grief and its expression is affirmed and legitimised. Therefore, ritual leaders have a function in orchestrating and ordering funerals but not in controlling and modifying the emotion felt and expressed, individually or corporately, within the ritual context.

---

6   Pastoral theologians such as Donald Capps (1981) and John Swinton (2007) and Old Testament scholars, Robert Davidson (1983) and Walter Bruggemann (1986) have in recent years written about the need to reclaim the psalms of lament as a key resource within the Judeo-Christian tradition as a means of enabling individuals and communities of faith to deal with significant experiences of loss.,

Ritual leaders during funerals, therefore, need to utilise the power invested in them with great discernment and sensitivity and as during co-construction manage the sacred space formed by those involved with wisdom (Pembroke 2004b) and integrity. Moreover, we require a good deal of self-awareness to gauge whether or not we are stilting the acknowledgement and expression of grief during co-construction or the funeral itself. Hence, the significance of supervision as normative for those working with the dying and bereaved to reflect on the interface between personal and inherited ways of dealing with loss and the behaviour of those the ritual leader is attempting to accompany and guide through their own journey of grief.

As well as having insight into the power and authority we possess within the process of ritualising the marking of the life and death of an individual and during the funeral itself, ritual leaders also require an understanding of the bereaved's need for us to be also be ourselves, human and vulnerable, while participating in the same activities. It requires a church representative not only to risk exposure to grief and pain but also to risk the possible acknowledgement of her own mortality and the mortality of those she loves.[7] This is both a challenge but potentially a relief for ritual leaders as we may with time, reflection and supervision reach a place where we no longer have to spend time and energy putting on, and keeping intact, a purely professional persona to repel all such 'threatening' feelings or experiences. Alan Horner (2005, 33), a Methodist minister, described in his poem *Vulnerability* our human resistance to such exposure:

> Strengthen your defences.
> Put on your armour.
> Strength is everything.

---

7 Acknowledgement yes, but total ownership probably never. We may understand we are mortal yet may spend a lifetime denying it or struggling with it; perhaps this is simply part of being a finite human being.

Raise the barricade.
Refuse the gift.
It is a Trojan horse
which once within
will have you open
to a hurting world.

Avoidance of Collusion: A Challenge to Theology and Practice
Increasingly, I encounter dying people who do not want their funeral to be sad. They want those attending to have a party, celebrate their life (and future resurrection if that is their belief) and while doing so they must not cry or wear black but be bedecked in bright clothes. Recently, a bereaved person said to me as we sought to co-construct an appropriate funeral for his partner: 'Selina didn't do death. We are not to talk of death or mourning during the funeral.' It is tempting to collude with such wishes to prevent those co-authoring the funeral and those participating in it, including ourselves, having to confront the harsh reality of death.

> The funeral is something that mourners may dread in anticipation because of the finality of the physical separation which it rightly expresses. However, it is important to have a public recognition of death and to provide for a reverential disposal of the body. (Ainsworth-Smith and Speck 1999, 99)

To collude in the denial of death during a funeral and in its co-construction is not only to ignore the significance of bereavement theory but it is to deny the theology which also informs our practice. Roger McGough (2006, 44) in his own inimitable tongue-in-cheek manner challenges this prevalent penchant for funerals to be purely celebratory in nature, ignoring the finality, the pain and confrontational nature of the death of a loved one. In fantasising about what he hopes his funeral will be like, he writes this:

I don't want any of that
'we're gathered here today
to celebrate his life, not mourn his passing.'
Oh yes you are. Get one thing straight,
You're not here to celebrate
but to mourn till it hurts.

I want wailing and gnashing of teeth.
I want sobs, and I want them uncontrollable.
I want women flinging themselves on
the coffin
And I want them inconsolable.

Don't dwell upon my past but on your future.
For what you see is what you'll be,
and sooner than you think.
So get weeping. Fill yourselves with dread.
For I am not sleeping. I am dead.

Setting aside McGough's egocentric desire for a feminine outpouring of grief, his poem has much to say to ritual leaders in terms of theological integrity and ritual practice. Part of the church representative's task in enabling meaningful funerals to be shared is to utilise 'the language of lament to deepen the awareness of pain and create supportive contexts for expressing "where our wounds hurt most"' (Anderson and Foley 1998, 117 who cite Nouwen [1982, 16–7]). However, to focus only on lament and loss during a funeral without thanksgiving or celebration is to deny the significance of the deceased's life to the mourners in the past, present and future and our belief, as church representatives, in resurrection.

Whether a funeral is overtly Christian and the love, mercy and compassion of God in Christ is proclaimed or not (as well as the Gospel being embodied in the actions, attitude and way of being and relating of the ritual leader) for a church representative to act with theological integrity the funeral requires to be shaped and informed by the Easter story. Paul Sheppy, a Baptist liturgist (2003), helpfully compares the Paschal mystery with van Gennep's tripartite understanding of rites of passage, including funerals. Within the sharing of this ritual there requires to be acknowledgement of death and the ending of what has been (Separation or Good Friday), a staying or waiting with the pain and sorrow tangibly felt (Transition or Easter Saturday) and a thanksgiving or celebration of a new but different life or existence for the deceased and the possibility of new beginnings for the bereaved (Re-aggregation or Easter Day). The responsibility for the management of the sacred space and the movement of the bereaved through such a process lies with the ritual leader (though different mourners will have a tendency to want to focus on one or other of the phases and/or move backwards and forwards between these aspects of the funeral). The hope of resurrection for the deceased and their incorporation into the Communion of Saints during a Christian funeral is overtly stated and thanksgiving for God's mercy and love articulated. For those (either dying or bereaved) who do not share these views and do not wish themselves or their loved one committed into God's love and care in the hereafter, the concept of the bereaved having a 'continuing bond' with the deceased (though a very different relationship) has parallels with the Christian concept of the Communion of Saints. In a sense the deceased are still part of the bereaved family's or community's lives – death may be the end of a physical relationship but a new type of relationship is formed and death, therefore, is not the absolute end of connections with the deceased. During a funeral, thanksgiving may be given for the formation of memories of life shared with the deceased in the past, the opportunity to recollect and share memories from different aspects of the deceased's life in the present moment and the ongoing integration of such memories into the individual and collective lives of the mourners in the future. Therefore, the life and way of living of the deceased continues to influence survivors from beyond the grave, for example, as benchmarks for living virtuous lives, guides for making difficult decisions and as silent listeners to the verbalised feelings and stories of survivors.

Significance of a Chaplain's Way of Being and Relating

Bereaved parents requested chaplaincy support because they perceived a church representative to have ritual authority but once they began to work with the ritual leader, it was the church representative's way of being and relating which significantly helped their spiritual needs to be met. In performing the many roles previously described, prior to and during ritual marking, it was the church representative's humanity, personhood and compassion that parents remembered not just what was said or done. '*He was so warm. It wasn't just a job to him*' (Mother 7). '*It was just the way he was ... em ... and he was actually, you could actually see he was kind of, he was, really upset as well*' (Mother 5). They also valued the ritual leader's steadfastness and willingness to stay with them as they expressed their feelings both during co-construction and the funeral itself. Chaplains did not shy away from strongly expressed emotion or confrontation with death.

The chaplain's approachability, sensitivity and warmth were considered highly significant. Ritual leaders by being themselves enabled parents to relax and be themselves. '*His whole manner*' (Father 8). '*it was just, yeah, it was just the way he was*' (Mother 8). '*Just the comfort you take from his character ... The way he is*' (Father 5).

Consequently, parents felt the church representatives were easy to relate to and felt valued and affirmed by their support. '*you weren't another burden, you were a person*' (Mother 7). Such experience of chaplaincy involvement was in direct contrast to what was expected by parents before meeting a church representative. '*There was never any awkwardness at all. I expected a lot more awkwardness and there was none of that*' (Father 7).

Informed by such reflections, an exploration of the personal qualities that enabled church representatives to be with, and relate to, bereaved parents in a meaningful way will be made. How church representatives can continue to work creatively and sensitively with the bereaved utilising such personal resources to the full over a sustained period will also be considered.

Gifts of Potential Ritual Leaders to Be Utilised, Developed and Sustained

Neil Pembroke, a pastoral theologian based in Australia, describes in *The Art of Listening* (2002) and *Working Relationships* (2004a) two essential gifts that a spiritual carer requires to offer others a depth of availability and attentiveness in the present moment. These attributes are compassion (associated with the notion of tenderness) and charm. From the findings of this study, it is also clear that the gifts of discernment and self-awareness are also important qualities to be possessed by church representatives working with the bereaved. These four innate abilities will now be briefly explored in relation to perceptions of bereaved parents.

Compassion

Pembroke (2002) describes the biblical notion of compassion as being associated with an instinctive, intimate relationship. In the world of the Israelites, compassion was linked with a Hebrew word group which indicated the type of feeling a mother has for the child of her womb. However, compassion, according to Paul, is more than a registering of an emotion; it is an expression of one's total being at the deepest level. The Greek word he uses, *splanchnon*, originally referred to the 'inward parts of the body' or to the womb (Pembroke 2002, 5). Compassion, thus, infers that the carer hears or observes someone's suffering and is deeply moved and responds in a tender and loving way. Compassion is more than empathy and acceptance, which are attitudes adopted towards another that convey availability. It is not a demeanour that can be assumed in certain circumstances and in certain relationships; compassion is a way of being.

For Pembroke (2002) the biblical understanding of compassion is closely allied to tenderness and, likewise, is a quality which is gifted rather than learnt and is observed in a carer's way of relating (in their physical as well as verbal response) to another. Pembroke (2002, 57) cites Thorne (1991, 75) when describing what tenderness may be.

> It is a word 'which means both vulnerable and warmly affectionate, easily crushed and merciful, not tough and sympathetic. It seems to incorporate both weakness and gentle strength, great fragility and great constancy.'

Charm

The concept of someone possessing charm is not always associated with positive connotations – a charmer being perceived as someone whose smooth talking influences the decision-making of another. However, Pembroke (2004a) highlights a more positive usage of the term, based on the work of Marcel (1950), which has relevance to our discussion of innate qualities possessed by ritual leaders, and identified by parents as having a significant bearing on the quality of bereavement care they delivered. Charm is a gift which enhances the ability of those who possess it to build up relationships with the bereaved and put them at their ease. Pembroke (2004, 79) defines a person of charm as:

> one who lives in and through a unity of *agape* and *eros*. *Agape* is expressed through an act of self-denial in which one's own needs and desires are temporarily suspended in order to attend to the other person. *Eros* produces a passion for life, for others, for God. It is a physical and spiritual energy that animates a person and renders her attractive and engaging.

We can only be charming as carers when we are truly being ourselves, not striving to be something which we are not. Charm, therefore, is a gift which is linked to consistency of character. It involves integrity – being the same person with the bereaved in the immediacy of their living room during co-construction, when relaxing at home with family or friends and when involved in sharing the funeral a few days later. We can only fully express God-given charm when we are able to accept ourselves for who we really are and live lightly with feelings of failure and shame.[8] The very presence of a chaplain who they perceived possessed a genuine interest in, and concern for, them helped bereaved parents feel able to relate to the church representative and express themselves as they needed to.

Discernment

In the Old Testament, the prophet Samuel, as a boy, displayed the ability to discern the voice of God but only with the direction of his mentor Eli and after learning from his previous experience (1 Samuel 3: 1–19). Jesus in his ministry displayed a depth of discernment in his relations with others, God and himself. He discerned when it was timely to listen (as a young man in the temple listening to his elders – Luke 2: 46) and when to speak (at the beginning of his ministry declaring his manifesto in the synagogue at Nazareth – Luke 4: 16–30) or act. Jesus was aware of when it was appropriate to give of himself (Matthew 9: 35 – speaks of Jesus' itinerant ministry as he moved between towns and villages teaching and responding to people's physical, emotional and spiritual needs) and when to receive (his anointing at Bethany in John 12) as well as when to stay and struggle (as in Gethsemane-Mark 14: 32–40) and when to leave (after teaching and healing in Capernaum all day Jesus saw more people coming to him and he asked his friends

---

8 Pembroke (2002) offers a helpful description of utilising such feelings, evoked by an awareness of being less than fully present with another, to aid potential self-growth and improve future practice.

to take him across the lake – Matthew 8: 18). His sensitivity in relating to others and tending to his own needs was not just due to trusting his own feelings or instinct. It was also grounded in his relationship with God and a desire to do God's will. Jesus' inner life and ability to distinguish God's voice in those voices around and within him was nurtured through regular retreat from interaction with others enabling solitary prayer and contemplation.

Bereaved parents perceived the chaplains who worked with them to possess a significant degree of discernment. For example, this natural ability was understood to help chaplains to gauge to what extent parents wanted to be involved in the co-construction of ritual marking and in the ritual itself, and whether it was appropriate for the chaplain to be present with parents at particular times, and for how long. The rock band The Clash (1982) sum up succinctly the key question which has come into the mind of every carer who has sought to sensitively support a bereaved individual or family – 'Should I stay or should I go now?' Moreover, church representatives require discernment in the decisions they make as to whether it is appropriate to verbally respond to parents' display of emotions or to remain silent and when they should change their role during co-construction, moving from being an unhurried supportive presence to being an interpretative guide, or during a funeral from being a mistress of ceremonies to a sustainer of grief. While some of these dilemmas may be answered by asking the bereaved what they need at that moment in time (though sometimes in the immediacy of their grief people don't know what's best or aren't able to articulate what they want), others cannot. A church representative, therefore, has to utilise his or her gift of discernment.

Discernment is a difficult concept to define. However, I would suggest within the context of offering spiritual care to the bereaved discernment is an ability to tune into the particular needs of an individual or family, enabling a loving, and in the long term, potentially healing response to be given.

In doing so, a church representative is also seeking to attend to the prompting of the One who is the source of love and to communicate that love to the best of her ability in a manner appropriate to the context and needs of each particular individual or family. Discernment cannot be acquired but it can be developed and honed through learning from experience and with the guidance of an insightful, prayerful other. Such ongoing deepening of our level of discernment requires attention to our inner self and, thus, discipline in making space for prayer and contemplation in our daily routine (Webster 2004–5). The practices of the faith tradition to which we belong (and those of others) may aid us in our ongoing quest to deepen our level of discernment (McCarthy 2000).

Discernment is also about being in touch with our gut feelings when we offer spiritual care, where so often we discover an inkling of another's spiritual needs and where the nudges and promptings of God may be recognised if we are attentive to them. If we become accustomed to listening to our inner being in solitude, we may be more prepared for listening to that which is stirred in our inner core when also relating to others. Thus, self-awareness is crucial in sifting through the different voices that inevitably arise within us when we encounter, death, raw grief and are involved in co-constructing and sharing in funerals. In seeking to utilise attributes of charm and compassion, which may enable God's love to be shared and the possibility of healing to occur, a ritual leader has to possess, nurture and utilise the gift of discernment. In seeking to be discerning a church representative has to be prepared to wait and suffer with the bereft and, thus, be actively attentive to each moment. For in doing so we may then hear something of the One whose voice we wait for when alone and with others. Acknowledging and attending to that voice will help us to respond in a loving way to the needs of those grieving and, as appropriate, our own.

Moreover, seeking to offer such care also sets any church representative up to fall short, as none of us, human as we are,

are as discerning and altruistic as Jesus, whose example we seek to follow. Therefore, as well as the courage to risk and to attempt to discern our appropriate response to the bereaved's perceived needs, offering spiritual care requires each of us to be gentle with ourselves; to be as accepting of the grace of God as much as we seek to share it with others.

Self-awareness

I have created you
in my own image.
Do you think that I
Crave for security?
Go out upon
a limb, the way I do:

Create a world,
be crucified,
and be obedient

Only to what you are.[9]
(From *The Good Boy* by Sydney Carter 1974, 22)

As has been suggested, much of what offering sensitive bereavement care involves is risk; the kind of risk which resonates with God's willingness to go out on a limb with us, and for us, and the rest of God's creation. However, as Carter points out, this first requires some awareness of whom and what we are, including having some insight into the natural abilities we do, and do not, possess. Therefore, as church representatives seeking to venture out on a limb and risk being available to, and then empowering, the bereaved we need to have some idea of the internal resources we have to utilise. As previously discussed, there is a need for an awareness of our own story, including any greater narratives that may shape that story and inform our motivation to become involved with those who are

---

9   The italics here are the author's.

vulnerable and distressed. Peter Speck (1978, 41), a former hospital chaplain, sums up the importance of a caring professional's self-awareness in supporting the bereaved. 'It is only as we feel sure of ourselves and our reactions that we feel able to be with someone as opposed to going to do things to that person.' Furthermore, there is also a need for openness to the possibility that during any relationship with a bereaved individual or family our story may be challenged, and indeed significantly changed, by what we encounter. This may not just affect how we approach our work as ritual leaders but it may also profoundly alter our interpretation of our own personal story, as well as our interpretation of the wider narratives that inform it.

Aspects of our personal story that require reflection to enhance our ability to relate sensitively to the bereaved include our:

Mortality (including previous losses, wounds and bereavements). Dealing with death and grief undoubtedly confronts any of us with our own mortality and the mortality of those we love. Moreover, how we deal with the wounds of others is dependent on how we have dealt, or not, with our own wounds. Muse (2000, 256–7), an American counsellor trainer, insightfully says this:

> The question is whether we will be wounded stealers or wounded healers. Self awareness is a key ingredient in determining the difference . . . .When recognised and owned by the pastor rather than projected onto others, woundedness is part of the wellspring of authentic motivations for ministry and can become a means of understanding and compassion for others. Unrecognised it becomes a barrier to love and effective ministry as pastors unconsciously seek to heal their woundedness by compulsively interfering with or ignoring what they perceive as similar wounds in others.

Limitations – personal and professional. As humans working in stressful and draining roles, it is essential ritual leaders are aware, or are capable of becoming increasingly aware, of their limitations. Each one of us has a limited supply of emotional, spiritual and physical resources which we can utilise to deal with particular situations and the cumulative effect of dealing with death and loss. How many of us have let bereaved families or funeral directors dictate our schedules rather than be honest about our own needs? It is all to easy to do but if we are to be human and open, able to risk and be sustainers of grief we too need time in which to be ourselves and attend to our needs. The bereaved perceive, as ritual leaders, our humanity and spirituality are at the heart of how we can create and share in meaningful funerals with them. We owe it to them and to ourselves to be honest about our needs as fellow fallible human beings.

There is also a requirement for church representatives to recognise the professional boundaries of our role and the roles of others with whom we work. We need to respect those boundaries, as encroaching on each others' roles, for example the funeral director's, leads to confusion for the bereaved as well as carers. Good communication between those involved in supporting a bereaved family, as well as with the family itself, is essential during the process of co-construction of a funeral and the ritual itself. Ritual leaders need to be able to recognise when seeking to meet the specific needs of a particular bereaved person or family that which is beyond our area of expertise or personal resources and be able to refer them to other colleagues, church members, their doctor or supportive, including counselling, agencies.

An important tool for developing self-awareness for ritual leaders is the use of supervision, mentoring and/or spiritual direction (see below). Even when we are aware that we may need support at specific times it requires energy and courage to seek appropriate help particularly if we are working in a local culture where being seen to do so is considered a sign of weakness and an inability to cope. Energy and initiative may be in short supply at a time when we are struggling. Therefore, it is even more imperative that regular support is proactively sought and put in place, if it is not offered.[10]

A Ritual Leader's Personal and Professional Development

Nurturing Ritual Leaders' Humanity and Spirituality
Bereaved parents interviewed perceived a chaplain's support of them to be emotional and spiritually draining for her. Such personal costs are paralleled in the ministry of Jesus as he met the needs of the bereaved and the sick, for example, we read in Mark 5: 26 that after Jesus responded to a woman with heavy menstrual bleeding that 'power had gone out of him'.

In James Wood's novel *The Book against God* (2003, 245–6), his central character Tom Bunting, listens intently to a recording of a live performance of a Beethoven concerto. So taken is Bunting with the beginning of the piece that he asks his wife if she could stop the record to allow him to enjoy again its first few chords. As he listened a second time Bunting hears not only the melody but also something more.

> Yet there was another sound, not musical. Something like a man sniffing. It was the pianist breathing! – heavy, almost impatient, as if he were wrestling with the music to secure its great medial serenity. The pianist was breathing quite hard through his nose as he wrestled with this sweet sound. It was the sound of hard work, but it was also the sound of existence itself – a man's ordinary breath, the give and take of the organism, our colourless wind of survival, the zephyr of it all. The evidence of human effort, of pain was intensely moving .

---

10   For many practitioners having the opportunity to approach a supervisor, mentor or spiritual director of their own choosing is preferable to being assigned one.

Like playing music, like staying with a melody that has been composed, being with another in distress is difficult and requires much effort and attention. Making our self available to the grief and searching of the bereaved, individually and corporately, is energy sapping work.

A key question, therefore, is how do church representatives sustain and nurture their emotional, physical, social and spiritual lives to repeatedly enter into situations and relationships where they are confronted with a myriad of emotions and an array of questions to which there are no easy answers? In this respect, the following are important for ritual leaders to consider.

Relationship with God and self

then he went up the hill by himself to pray. It had grown late and he was there alone. (Matthew 14: 23)

Both while listening during co-construction and when stories are recounted and enacted during funerals, the church representative involved is experiencing and holding pain – for a while. However, there comes a point when there is a need to hand over those feelings of loss and dereliction onto a Greater Being whose shoulders are far broader and infinitely more able to carry the cumulative weight of such expressed emotion. The pain of others can touch and move us, facilitate reflection and growth, but also has the potential to overwhelm us over a period of time. It is not ours to keep but to hand over, not just so that we, as ritual leaders, have sufficient spiritual and emotional resources available to make room for, and be attentive to, the pain of the next bereaved person we care for (and the next!). More than that, we, as human beings, need enough of both for ourselves so that the rest of life can be lived fully. Yet in the effort of each moment being with, and being receptive to, the pain of another and of self is the promise of something more, something shared and something other.

The present moment is significant, not as the bridge between past and future, but by reason of its contents, contents which can fill our emptiness and become ours if we are capable of receiving them. (Hammarskjold 1966, 67–8)

In receiving these moments as gifts – as moments of grace – our lives may be enhanced, even paradoxically in the midst of death and grief. Subsequent reflection on what we have experienced during funerals and their co-construction may improve our understanding of how we relate to others in particular situations of distress. Indeed, contemplation only has real meaning when it deepens our engagement with others (Marcel 1950, cited by Pembroke 2002). Moreover, such reflection as well as increasing our self-awareness also aids our ongoing journey into the mystery of God. A deepening of understanding of self, of what we can make available to others and of God's involvement in our lives and in our encounters, is an ongoing sojourn. Pembroke (2002, 218) helpfully puts it this way while also making a comparison with learning psychotherapeutic techniques as a sole means of meeting people's spiritual needs.

A person with the requisite ability and diligence can master interventions in a few short years. It takes a life-time, however, to even begin to grasp what it means to share in a real meeting with another human being.

Opportunities for creativity and depth of insight may be enhanced by the company of a supervisor/mentor or spiritual director along the way.

Many people do not know themselves, because they proudly believe they can give birth to themselves. The fact is that none of us can reveal ourselves to ourselves, unless we first reveal ourselves to another. (Quoist 1986, 19 cited by Stoter 1995, 151)

While supervision and spiritual direction could be considered as two separate activities, both involve a confidential relationship with a wise and discerning other who can potentially aid us, amongst other things, to grow in our knowledge of self. Spiritual direction is more concerned with 'understanding ourselves in the light of God' (Goodacre 1983, 115), whereas supervision has managerial, educative (including possible ongoing theological reflection) and supportive aspects (Moore and Levison 2003).

Such potentially illuminating relationships also contain possibilities of recognising and owning our own needs within the helping relationships we are involved in. Cooper-White (2004, 110) emphasises the importance of this dimension of self-awareness for carers:

> The capacity to become *aware* of one's own feelings and then to consider in a reflective vein what such feelings might be communicating – about both one's own needs for healing and the needs of the helpee – are the essential skills for . . . caring genuinely and empathetically for another.

Irvine (1997 with reference to McFadyen [1990]) suggests that our identities are shaped in relationship with others as well as by exploration of our inner selves. The movement towards personal wholeness and integration is seeking a balance between being attentive to these two contrasting worlds. There is, therefore, a need for chaplains to attend to the world of being and waiting, recognising and responding to voices from within and mindful of the part of our self which gratifies our egos through doing, achieving and receiving affirmation from others. Giving priority to this second aspect of our makeup results in our identity, for ourselves and others, being equated with activity and responding to others' needs. There is a potential threat to our health if our identity becomes tied up in our role rather than in whom we really are. Much energy may be utilised in keeping up the pretence, with little left for listening and responding to personal needs.

In developing self-awareness and, thus, our spirituality, on our own or with another, is again to risk. It is to risk being open to new understandings of self and God discovered within and from encounters with others. Au and Cannon (1995, 22) helpfully cite the mystic and theologian Teilhard de Chardin on this issue – 'Let us leave the surface, and without leaving the world, plunge into God.' As the risk involved in seeking to be available for others and letting go of funeral ownership, the risk of entering into the unknown places of our inner selves and having to dealing with pain and fear that is awakened within us, as well as possibilities for further enlightenment, is also very real. Hammarskjold (1966, 65) articulates this ongoing inward search as 'The longest journey.'

Such seeking, like the delivery of spiritual care, therefore, requires a church representative to have courage as well as a sense of commitment to prayer and reflection. It also means that ritual leaders require a lightness of touch with ourselves. As Pembroke reminds us (2004, 30): 'nurture of the self requires patience. Harshness towards the self stunts growth'. Thus, perhaps the most important aspect of our relationship with God and ourselves, which enables us to make ourselves available for bereaved parents, is a belief in God's love for us. To love others requires of us that we feel we are loved and are loveable in our own right. Muse (2000, 258) insightfully puts it this way: '*Belovedness* is what provides the most essential ingredient for healthy psychological development that leads to compassion and conscience.'

Play and the company of significant others

To meet our spiritual needs in a rounded way, time and attention must be given in a ritual leader's life to play. The sense of playfulness required to enable bereavement care to be meaningfully provided is beautifully depicted in a Punch cartoon which parodies an illustration found in *The House at Pooh*

Corner (Milne 1928, 104). Winnie the Pooh and some of his friends are standing on a bridge over a stream playing at pooh-sticks. The caption underneath the cartoon reads 'I'm fed up of playing poohsticks let's go down the arcade and get ourselves tattooed.' Whether poohsticks or decorating our bodies is our favourite pastime or not, play and enabling the expression of the child within us is an important way of recharging our spiritual batteries. Play offers a balance in life to the intensity and layers of loss experienced in supporting the bereaved. However, making time in which to play, for play's sake, is counter to prevalent Western, including ecclesial, cultures of doing and achieving. Fostering a life which is well-rounded and finding a balance between work and leisure is important for ritual leaders as is making time to enjoy our personal relationships. In the company of those who love us and accept as we are, and not for what we can do or be for them, there is opportunity for restoration (Herrick and Mann 1998). In the love we receive from others, we may glimpse something of the unconditional love of God for whom we are a 'beloved' son or daughter and in whom God takes 'delight' (Matthew 3:17).

In responding to the ever-changing spiritual needs of others in the present moment there is the challenge for us as ritual leaders to attend to our own dynamic spiritual journey and needs which also, as we are as much human as those we care for, change through our experience and sharing of life with others.

The shaping and development of a ritual leader's personhood and practice

As well as being a source of motivation and inspiration, a church representative's faith may be a potential source of comfort and solace. The Christian tradition offers a variety of ethical and theological perspectives, derived from biblical sources, which gives a ritual leader a framework to utilise in engaging with, and interpreting, the complexities of human experience. A belief system is, therefore, required which informs not only our intellectual reasoning but which also shapes who we are and how we act out our faith. Being part of such a tradition over a period, enables a *habitus* to occur – 'a disposition of the mind and heart from which action flows naturally, in an unself-conscious way' (Forrester 2000, 5). A church representative is, thus, able to work with integrity in a secular society (including hospitals and hospices) in supporting the bereaved (who invariably will not have a church-orientated faith) and co-construct meaningful funerals with them because 'their own identity has at its centre a theology funded by the Christian narrative' (Lyall 2001, 163). Stephen Pattison (1988, 16), a practical theologian based in Cardiff, is more prescriptive: 'pastoral carers should maintain a Christian vision, a spiritual life and sense of being rooted, grounded and orientated towards God, whatever the means they use to undertake their caring'.

Underpinning such aspirations of putting our theology into practice with integrity, as we co-author and share in funerals meaningful to those who are not Christian, is faithfulness (White 2002). Being faithful, according to White, in our day-to-day living, our relating at home and at work is the key to maintaining our humanity and identity within our postmodern context of rapid social change and fragmentation. Faithfulness does not resist change and personal growth, but enables each one of us to hold onto the essence of who we are and how we interact with others and God. How do any of us maintain our faithfulness, or indeed our desire to be faithful? White (2002, 88) makes a positive and helpful response to this question:

> The sustained will to be faithful is best formed within a relationship to God embodied in a character-forming community and set of social practices. This relationship with God may or may not be explicitly realized in these practices; nonetheless, the specific value of a confessing and worshipping community, forming the character of a confessing and worshipping self, certainly needs to be recognised.

Our identities as individual human beings do have an essential degree of constancy and yet evolve over time. Therefore, having some awareness of how our identity may be reshaped and re-formed by being in contact with, and open, to the stories of others is important for ritual leaders. However, so too is, paradoxically, endeavouring to hold onto the essence of who we are and what fundamentally motivates and inspires us to be who we are becoming and do what we will do.

> This pattern is rooted in God. God's being is dynamic, but he does not lose any part of it within that dynamism. God holds his own experience of change within his own being. This helps define God's identity. In this way God is both responsive and essentially unchanging. (White 2002, 150)

Reflection on interviews with bereaved parents has revealed that an individual's personal attributes are central to her capacity to fulfil a ritual leader's role. Clearly, a church representative's personhood informs her practice and, when open to reflection on experience, a ritual leader's practice may reshape or re-form elements of her character or identity. Thus, a church representative's personal growth and professional development are closely linked. There is a need to prioritise the sustaining and nurturing of the personhood and spirituality of ritual leaders by national churches and local faith communities, as well as by the church representatives themselves, to enable meaningful funerals to be offered and to further develop relevant and creative approaches. Therefore, proactive measures are required to enable ritual leaders to mature and develop as persons as well as reflective practitioners. Similar observations are made by the Church of Scotland's Board of Ministry in a report to the General Assembly entitled *Ministers of the Gospel* (Church of Scotland 2000, 17/24):

> those called to the ministry of Word and Sacrament, ministers (and other church representatives involved in

co-creating and sharing in funerals with the bereaved)[11] of the Gospel in the 21st century must be reflective practitioners, collaborative leaders and formative learners . . . the theology and practice of ordained ministry . . . requires a clear capacity and commitment among all ministers of the Gospel to deep reflection, genuine collaboration and continuing formation as persons in Christ and practitioners in ordained ministry.

Thus, in order for chaplains to nurture their own humanity and spirituality and to reflect on the relationship between their theology and practice an ongoing commitment to making time and space to do so is required.[12] Built into the rhythm of work and play, ministering to and receiving from, requires an attentiveness, both individually and corporately, to our inner worlds and our interactions with others, and what of God may be glimpsed in both. By co-creating and sharing in appropriate funerals with the bereaved and by then reflecting on such experiences, church representatives not only have the opportunity to learn how to improve our care for such families. We also have the opportunity to learn more about ourselves. Put another way, in the terms of a hermeneutical approach (Capps 1984) to providing spiritual care there is the opportunity to let encounters with others read us, if we are prepared to risk developing our own self-understanding through ongoing reflection on practice.

Who we are and what we believe informs our practice but equally our practice can influence what we believe, which in turn will inform our future care. Jacobs (1988, 21) describes how close attention to the stories we hear in caring relationships may have significant implications for our unfolding theology

---

11 The words in parentheses are mine and are not found in the *Ministers of the Gospel* report.

12 For a helpful schema to aid reflective practice see Schon (1983). Carroll (1986) offers a pertinent exploration of Schon's approach within the field of ministry and Lyall (2001) likewise, within the particular context of pastoral care.

listening is the precursor to understanding, to interpreting, and to help the teller interpret (albeit in the simplest terms) the significance of the story now, in this place, at this time, and with this listener. There may be times when listening to the narrative in this way will go beyond pastoral care, to the making of a personal theology.

The theology of each ritual leader is as particular to each of us as our individual characters and personhood. However, in order for church representatives to be able to co-create and share in funerals which will be meaningful to the bereaved in our postmodern world our beliefs will be significantly influenced by God's love rather than being bound by dogma. Our theology will not only shape how we relate to the bereaved but it will also inform our approach to constructing and performing funerals as well as their content. However, we should neither seek to impose our beliefs on the bereaved nor be so rigid in our mode of practice as to prevent a loving, compassionate response to the particular needs of a family. What is required is an embodiment of God's love in response to pain and grief; a love that involves 'open-ness, vulnerability, availability and confession (when we get it wrong)'[13] (Nouwen 1969, 33).

James Fowler (1995 and 1996) formed, from his engagement with psychological perspectives of the development of self in childhood, a schema for describing stages of faith which a person may sequentially inhabit at different times in their lives. Working with the bereaved in a postmodern context requires church representatives to be mature in their faith and have some experience of dealing with pain and suffering in their own lives. Fowler's (1996, 65) description of 'Conjunctive faith' (which he feels may be discovered and lived out in early midlife and beyond) articulates the approach to faith that ritual leaders

---

13   The words in parentheses are mine not Nouwen's.

require to provide sensitive spiritual care and to retain a sense of personal integrity.

> In the transition to the Conjunctive stage one begins to make peace with the tension arising from the realization that truth must be approached from a variety of different directions and angles of vision . . . faith must begin to come to terms with indissoluble paradoxes; the strength found in apparent weakness; the leadership that is possible from the margins of society and groups but not from the centre; the immanence *and* the transcendence of God.

In short, ritual leaders require a faith that can live creatively with paradox and tension, for example, during funerals a ritual leader holds paradoxical roles (as mistress of ceremonies and as a sustainer of grief) sharing an event which has ambiguous aims (to physically disconnect the bereaved from the deceased yet also simultaneously affirm continuing bonds). Church representatives seeking to co-construct and share in funerals with the bereaved also require a theological understanding of ministry, and sense of self, that does not require us to be always in control and the centre of ritual attention. Whether a prospective ritual leader has such a faith perspective and depth of self-awareness (or the potential for both) should be thoroughly explored at an interview for appointment (as a salaried church representative or as gifted member of a congregation) both for their well-being and that of the bereaved persons they may work with.

In conclusion, the natural qualities a ritual leader possesses are central to her ability to relate sensitively to the bereaved and construct and share in meaningful funerals with them. Prospective ritual leaders have to possess compassion and tenderness, charm and discernment. They are required to be people of integrity and mature in faith and self-awareness. They have to possess the ability to be available and attentive to others, but also to be able to leave and let go. Those seeking to co-construct and share in funerals with the bereaved need to possess the desire to glimpse something of God in their daily encounters but not seek to be God-like; omnipresent and omni-competent. They must be willing to give of self but be able to hold onto what is the essence of their unique self. They need to be team players – open to the work of the Other and respectful of the role and abilities of others. Candidates to become ritual leaders can have worked at developing their self-awareness, honed their counselling skills and reflected on their previous practice to enable past experience to inform future care. However, without possessing inherent gifts which enable connections with the bereaved times of grief and loss to be made, the care they may offer will be superficial and impersonal.

7

Co-construction of Funerals and Opportunities for the Church

Introduction

Religion is still closely connected with death, even if it is only acknowledged by the presence of the minister and the singing of hymns.

(Murray 2002, 26)

For many in postmodern Western society who consider the church as otherwise irrelevant and somewhat archaic, at a time of bereavement her representatives still have the capacity to be of great significance in helping the bereaved to mark the life and death of a deceased loved one. The British historian and broadcaster David Starkey, while being interviewed about his attitude to faith and ritual, offers insight into this prevalent contemporary perspective:

> He (Starkey) is an atheist. Priests are just 'silly, camp non-sense'. But he wanted one when his father died. 'I wanted someone to say the words, 'the ashes to ashes', the 'dust to dust', the half-comprehensible language, musical, sono-rous, powerful, and triggering memories of Grandma's prayer book. That's what I wanted at that point. I couldn't care less whether I believed in the resurrection or the life after death – that's what I wanted'. (Deveney 2006, 16)

Church representatives, whether they work in community or institutional settings, are still regarded by many who are not confessional Christians to be the most culturally appropriate

163

persons to perform a funeral.[1] Church representatives are perceived to have ritual authority – possessing the skills, knowledge, training and experience to help give them or a family member 'a decent send off' (Kelly 2007). It may well be that in their locality a church representative has built up credibility for sharing meaningful funerals with the bereaved whatever their social background, beliefs or life experience. If the bereaved do not know her personally, neighbours, family, members of staff or funeral directors who do, may recommend such an approachable church representative to them. There will be some bereaved families who may feel an affinity with a local congregation or the church universal due to historical attachment, even in previous generations and, thus, feel it is appropriate, even their right, to seek ritual support from her representatives. Others may feel guilty or hypocritical for doing so because of non-attendance, doubts or difficulty with dogma.

The bereaved bring with them into a relationship with a ritual leader their past experience of the church, her clergy and her members. This may profoundly impact on the degree of sharing and storytelling during co-construction and, therefore, influence the content, form and atmosphere of the funeral shared. Writing after years of experience as a Church of England priest Wesley Carr (1985, 28) describes well the hesitancy and anxiety of parishioners approaching a local minister for help with a funeral:

---

1 There are, however, a growing number of alternative individuals, groups or organisations which are not affiliated with a particular faith community available for the bereaved to turn to if they want help with creating a funeral, religious or otherwise, for example, The Humanist Association for life-centred, non-religious funerals. Interfaith ministers or celebrants are available in different parts of the country and organisations such as 'Life-ceremonies' (www.life-ceremonies.com) provide help in preparing and performing funerals as well as counselling and support. Other groups such as the 'New Bereavement and Funeral Trust' provide training courses for individuals who have some experience in working with the dying and bereaved to become funeral advisors – people who offer the bereaved information and advice about the practicalities of arranging a funeral.

They vaguely know what they want but usually cannot articulate it very clearly. . . . They are trapped between doing what they feel is proper and what they instinctively feel is odd – going to the church and the vicar.

Where an individual or family's experience of the church has been negative; time, effort and sensitivity may be required to establish a relationship of trust where openness and honest expression feels permitted. It can be difficult for both parties when past church-related wounds of grieving relatives are reopened as they feel obliged by circumstance to seek the help of a church representative. In the hands of a skilled and non-judgemental carer, there are opportunities for healing of those hurts and for the church, and the God whom she seeks to embody, to be experienced in a different light.

Co-construction and Opportunities for the Church to Learn

In our postmodern world there is much mourning within church circles over the lack of a shared language and common metaphors and images in society to describe humanity's experiences and aspirations relating to mortality, death and beyond. This certainly can prove challenging to those who seek to create relevant funerals with bereaved persons who have little or no knowledge or understanding of the Judeo-Christian story yet wish the support of a church representative in ritual marking. However, alongside the challenges of working in a postChristian context come opportunities for the church.

The model of working with the bereaved to co-construct funerals for their loved one not only enables many of their spiritual needs to be met but it also affords the chance for the church, in the form of her ritual representative, to grow and learn. There are opportunities to learn from the bereaved how to provide spiritual, and not only pastoral, care where the bereaveds' struggle to make sense of life, death and suffering takes into account a range of reference narratives and not just the Judeo-Christian story. Reflection on practice gives the opportunity to utilise the experience of what we have heard and shared to influence our theology and, thus, future practice. Not only do ritual leaders have the chance to wrestle with theology and theodicy by their involvement in co-construction but also to learn new phrases and metaphors which convey something of the mysteries of life, death and suffering as well as images of God and an afterlife. The bereaved as they struggle to make sense of the death of their loved one use a variety of sources which are part of their own everyday experience to articulate their ideas and beliefs. In hearing, affirming and using such insights and word-pictures we have the opportunity not only to personalise individual funerals but also to inform our own personal spiritual development. Moreover, in doing so we are deepening the church's understanding of postmodern culture and how people in wider contemporary society relate to suffering, death and God. Such perceptions expressed in a variety of images, gestures and words may also be offered to others as they struggle to articulate their own interpretation of such mysteries. Thus, the bereaved who the church seek to support may not only potentially receive but give, if we in the church are prepared to be open to such gifts. Those who are vulnerable can be our teachers enabling we who offer ritual support not only an extension of resources for other bereaved persons (whether actively involved in a faith community or not) but also an enrichment of the existing liturgies which mark the life and death of individuals, communities and relationships. The articulation of 'hidden needs and life experiences' are gifts of word-pictures which may inform our liturgies which are often 'over-narrow and impoverished' (Graham 2000, 100) in relation to rites of passage.

In adopting such an approach to ritual construction with those who are not active members, the church, in the form of her representatives, is perceived not to have overriding control or ownership of funerals. Neither is the church understood to impose an alien language, stories and actions but is experienced as being prepared to risk, to be open and take seriously the story, and means of expressing that story, of the bereaved. Therefore, what the ritual leader embodies is the church as learner not just teacher, the church as listener and not just teller, the church as receiver and not just giver and the church as vulnerable and not omnipotent. Thus, the church through the work of her ritual representatives may adopt a 'listening posture', and the possibilities associated with it, rather than just the more traditional stance of proclamation (Scott 2000, 18). This has implications not only for how the church is perceived to act but for what the church may be. Webster (2002, 128) puts it this way:

> My vision of the Christian identity is that it is not simply the *foundation*, the jumping off point, for our activity. It is also the *product* of our activity. We may undertake certain activities because we are Christian but in undertaking these, the nature of our Christian identity changes. We see new visions of God and of humanity, and have to reconceptualize our faith accordingly. Identity and experience are locked in a mutually enhancing cycle – changed by one another. In the encounter between church and society, the trick is to ensure that Christianity is neither lost in translation, nor left unaffected by it.

In the process of helping those for whom the Christian story is not the predominant framework through which they interpret or engage with the world and their experiences of it, church representatives encounter the stories of those who seek to understand and deal with their loss through other influences. The faith and beliefs of church workers are, therefore, exposed to new stories in their encounters with the bereaved and potentially new ways of understanding their beliefs and

way of practising. Willows and Swinton (2000, 15) put it
this way:

> Formative experiences, for example, such as suffering,
> alienation, chaos and confusions (including bereave-
> ment),[2] are invariably communicated and interpreted
> through the stories people tell about themselves and their
> experiences. . . . it could be argued that the essence of
> faith itself has to do with the possibility of encountering
> stories that transform who we are and the way in which
> we see the world.

Part of what any church representative may learn more about
by working with the bereaved is their human mortality.
Through an openness to being confronted with the inevitability of death and loss by aiding the ritual marking of others'
mortality there are opportunities for the church, locally and
globally, to develop a more healthy attitude to death within its
own body. Streets (1996, 182–3) offers a reminder that funerals
not only confront us with our mortality but also offer us a
means by which we can learn individually and corporately how
to live with death:

> The art of dying and death is reviewed, remembered, and
> learned in subtle ways at the funeral as people gather and
> participate in the rituals that organize and give meaning to
> death . . . .All funerals are also about our own life and death.
> How we grieve and cope with loss throughout life is
> reflected in and influenced by the way we bury our dead.

Reflection on the practice of chaplains working with
bereaved parents to create and share in meaningful funerals for
their babies also reveals the significance of lament in the practice

---

2   The words in parentheses here are mine.

of bereavement care and sensitive funeral constriction. This is affirmation of the importance of the role of lament in the authentic life, worship and witness of the church. Lament resonates with the contemporary struggle to make sense of the violence, terror and uncertainty lived with in our postmodern age where the average citizen feels helpless and powerless in the face of a perceived terrorist threat to Western social, political and economic stability. Regular expression of lament is a necessity for a worshipping community to be faithful to its biblical roots, retain theological integrity and have relevance in a world infused by layers of loss and an individual and collective search for meaning.

> A theology that has no place for lament is left only with thin, inadequate murmurings. The covenantal relationship is reduced to a mere shell, manoeuvred about with smoke and mirrors rather than serious and faithful engagement. As Brueggemann says, 'Covenant minus lament is finally a practice of denial, cover-up and pretense . . .'
>
> The laments ground the practice of pastoral care in the reality of human experience. (Jones 2007, 55)

As part of the practice of the spiritual care of bereaved parents and families whose loved ones die in hospitals and hospices many chaplains perform non-religious funerals. Other church representatives working in a range of institutional and community contexts do likewise. As I have attempted to show the co-construction and shared performance of such rituals are rooted in, and shaped by, the theology, spirituality and personhood of the church representative involved, whether the funerals are explicitly religious or not. As a reader and fellow (or potential fellow) ritual leader you may feel you could not conduct a funeral which is not explicitly Christian; your theological integrity does not allow you to do so. I believe neither perspective is right nor wrong but perceive both perspectives to be theologically informed.

I have attempted to weave theology, explicitly and implicitly, into my exploration of what makes funerals meaningful. I hope I have shown that within the privilege of co-constructing and sharing in funerals with the bereaved much theology is being done and reflected upon by both ritual leader and grieving families, whether they call themselves religious or not. There may be no specific end product or schema to such theologising for doing theology in such a way is far from systematic. It is fragmentary but nonetheless real and meaningful. Moreover, if we dare, such theologising may not just inform our future practice as ritual leaders but it may also be an opportunity for the church to learn – not just about how to sensitively care for the bereaved but more about God, herself and how she relates, or not, to the surrounding world. Duncan Forrester (2005, ix) put it this way:

> Theological fragments, as I understand them, arise from, and relate to, specific situations, problems, contexts, issues and communities. But often insights from one specific situation are found to be of more general relevance. A theology of fragments hopes to contribute to throwing some light on what is going on, and challenging to constructive and faithful practice today.

Co-construction and Opportunities for the Church to Meet the Needs of the Wider Community

Opportunities to Empower the Bereaved
Scot's lyricist Mike Scott (2006) in his song *Strange Arrangement* sums up well the church's historical movement away from Christ's approach to care of the vulnerable and disempowered in relation to her representatives' seeming need to control the content and form of funerals: 'I exchanged the power of love for the love of power.' Emily Dickinson (1999, 60) beautifully describes the utilisation of such power by a clergyman to ensure

control over the bereaved, including expression of their grief, in her poem 'There's been a death.'

> The Minister – goes stiffly in –
> As if the House were His –
> And He owned all the Mourners – now–
> And the little Boys – besides –

Control enables a church representative to keep grief and pain at bay but renders already powerless mourners further bereft. On the other hand, entering into a relationship which enables the bereaved to be as they need to be, to share their story and help to co-author an appropriate funeral for their loved one (if they wish) is about affirming and empowering those who grieve. It is a movement back towards the power, and empowering nature, of love. Such an approach seeks to help the bereaved experience sacred spaces, places of sanctuary and new possibilities. The space negotiated between a church representative and the bereaved should make an individual or family feel safe, held and supported and that they have permission to express and experience pain. At the same time, such spaces should be places of hope and potential healing where new meanings in life which incorporate the experience of loss and suffering may be glimpsed and the realisation of personal mortality may be experienced. These sacred spaces are not just found in the place of safety or holding which may be experienced during a funeral but in a relationship of trust and openness formed during the process of co-construction of funerals. Both are temporary havens created when the bereaved need shelter and permission to be as they need to be but also have the aim of helping those who grieve to discover, with time, the seeds of new beginnings and meanings. This may include discoveries about God and that the expression of lament to, and doubts about, God are permissible. Furthermore, in such contexts the bereaved may find hitherto hidden inner resources and strengths, including an ability to live with loss and grow through it.

> In the practice of caring, the sacred locates itself in the places of *lodgement* and *germination*.[3] . . . The words *holding environment* carry spiritual meanings: the care as a sanctuary from destructive forces and a launching pad for new life. (van Katwyk 2002, 118)

Co-constructing funerals is not a method of creating ritual which denies or abnegates the power that church representatives undoubtedly possess and utilise during their relationships with the bereaved. However, such an approach to shaping funerals empowers the bereaved not only to regain control in a situation where hitherto they felt powerless but also to be creative, feel they are doing the best that they possibly can for their deceased loved one and be involved in meaningful and fulfilling activity. Such use of power by ritual leaders resonates with themes in feminist pastoral theology:

> Women find the exercise of power more satisfying if it simultaneously enhances the lives of others. Roles and careers traditionally assigned to women presuppose such attention to developing and nurturing others' gifts: motherhood, teaching, nursing. Enabling others is a central goal of women in ministry. Yet this is real power. (Fischer 1989, 142 cited by Graham 2002, 184)

Entering into caring relationships with the bereaved where the aim is to help them create meaningful funerals out of their experience of loss and life shared with the deceased is an opportunity for men and women in ministry, lay or ordained, to learn about the compassionate use of such power. In so

---

3 In the words of T. S. Elliot, without a 'place of lodgement and germination', our world remains 'waste and void' (van Katwyk 2002, 112 citing Elliot 1964, 172).

doing, there is a potential meeting with that which is vulnerable and paradoxically powerful – self, others and the Divine.

> The power of compassion is divine: the compassion expressed in simple acts of acknowledging each others' fear and pain, standing with a baby with colic, caring for a friend dying with AIDS, acknowledgement, without diminishment, the pain that others feel; the power of saying: 'Your pain is real, your cries are heard, your anger is just, and along with you are many others who mourn and rage.' The power of compassion and anger is holy. (Welch 1990, 173)

In such experiences of shared vulnerability during collaborative working not only are there opportunities of glimpsing the Divine but finding shared fulfilment in creating something meaningful and unique together. In the co-creation of, and sharing in, meaningful funerals with the bereaved there is, thus, opportunity for the church to incarnate Jesus' way of living and relating as well as central tenants of his teaching; offering healing and hope to the vulnerable and marginalised, whatever strata of society they belong to, by empowering them and in doing so risking ourselves.

Opportunities to Aid Others in Their Search for Meaning

Human beings are meaning-seeking creatures; we crave narratives that have a beginning and an end – something that we rarely encounter in everyday life.

Armstrong (2006b, 29) is right; so often in life our narratives and those of whom we love are cut short or are inextricably altered by illness, accident, divorce or death. This leaves those bereft searching for meaning, reason and purpose in such events or processes.

With the coming of the postmodern era, due to a lack of shared traditional religious and cultural norms individuals and families increasingly have become anxious and confused in the face of having to deal with death and dying and their associated rituals. There is 'an insecurity resolved by medicine, by commercial undertakers and by bureaucratic welfare systems. As physical and financial beings people welcomed this, but as meaning-creating and self-determining individuals many felt lost' Walter (1994, 26).

In a postmodern context where external authorities are being rejected, a co-creative approach by church representatives to the shaping of funerals is an attempt to redress this imbalance. Co-construction enables the sharing of cultural norms, information and resources (sacred and secular) which empower decision-making. During such a process, the ritual leader involved facilitates the articulation of feelings and experience, offers an opportunity for the bereaved to search for meaning in their experience and aids the normalisation of grief. In a broader context, the church in our postmodern world, where people are seeking a relevant means by which to express their response to tragedy and trauma (at a personal or global level), has a role, which could be further developed, in facilitating rituals appropriate to the spiritual, and not merely religious needs, of local, national and international communities. For the church to be able to do so her ritual leaders need to be prepared to risk listening to, and working with, those who are not active in local faith communities. This would involve letting go of power and the control of ritual construction and using the ritual authority invested in them by communities with discernment and humility. Here is an opportunity for the church to build up relationships with those who have no particular faith attachment and create contexts in which the expression of grief and search for meaning feels permissible. Through the process of co-construction, the rituals formed and shared will emerge from the real experience and needs of ordinary people (in funerals, memorial services and other ritual markings). The church is ideally placed to help facilitate this process, as it has to offer an array of rich human, symbolic and written resources from within its various traditions. Webster (2002, 122) offers valuable insight:

> Those who are well practised in the design of worship
> and liturgy could be seen as being gifted with a rare
> generic skill: the use of the language of ritual to create
> dramatic and moving forms of expression which enable
> the articulation of truths which cannot be articulated in
> any other way ... the use of ritual and the deployment of
> the symbolic are enormously important for building
> emotional resilience and health, both for individuals and
> communities.

Putting such a vision into practice would involve utilising the time, talents and energy, of not only paid church workers but also of laity who possess the appropriate gifts. (Such a scheme is currently, for example, being explored within the Church of Scotland). Ritual and its co-construction following deaths which impact on families and communities, local and global, should be made more of a priority in the work and witness of the church. Training, support, supervision and the encouragement of ongoing personal and spiritual re-formation, including regular theological reflection on practice, therefore, also needs to be a norm for those acting as ritual leaders.

Utilising our Religious Resources Creatively

Utilising the Bible as a rich literary resource and not only as a religious one, is something poets and playwrights are well acquainted with but as yet ritual leaders have been shy to do likewise. The bereaved interviewed found resources from the Judeo-Christian tradition being made available to them, along with others from a variety of secular literary genres, helpful in aiding the co-construction of relevant funerals. Poetry and prose written hundreds of years ago which became canonical texts articulate a human response to love, loss and longing which helped many bereaved parents without church affiliation to articulate their experience, feelings and questions at a time when they found it hard to find their own words.

It is interesting to note that though the majority of parents would not have called themselves religious nearly every co-constructed funeral had a religious element within it (at the parents' behest). For some only a brief reference to God or an afterlife in a prayer or a blessing felt appropriate but for others their Christian beliefs pervaded the whole of the funeral. It is important, therefore, that when working to co-create meaningful funerals we do not sideline religious language or resources when empowering the bereaved to engage with the mysteries of life, death and eternity.[4] For even those who label themselves as non-religious may choose familiar words, prayers, hymns and biblical readings (e.g., from their childhood) from the Christian tradition to help express their feelings, longings and experience within ritual marking.

Dispelling Myths about the Church

The bereaved approaching and then working with a church representative to co-create and share in a funeral for their deceased loved one often do not have an interest in an ongoing relationship with the church worker nor the church. They seek the help of someone whom they regard as culturally appropriate to aid them with ritual marking and who has the training and experience to do so appropriately.

However, those church representatives prepared to respect the beliefs, experience and feelings of those who are not familiar with the Christian metanarrative can and do make a positive impression on the bereaved. Although it may not be the ritual

---

4   Grant et al. (2004) make a similar point in their study, in relation to patients who were living with advanced cancer and non-malignant disease, discussing their spiritual issues and needs. They discovered patients who considered themselves non-religious also often utilised religious language to articulate spiritual issues in their lives as they approached death.

leader's primary motivation for supporting the bereaved, their way of being, relating and sharing in funerals may make the bereaved think again about their perception of the church and the faith her representatives embody. Parents with no church connection, in the study reflected upon, had very negative expectations of meeting and being supported by one of her representatives. Such assumptions were dispelled once they had shared their stories and ritual action with a chaplain. In Newbigin's (1988) terminology, the church representative, especially through her personhood and way of being present, offered an interpretative 'lens' through which many parents perceived the life and work of the church anew. For most parents this lens was very different from the one they expected to encounter.

Opportunities to Help Regulate Grief in Contemporary Society

By utilising the approach of co-construction for the formation of funerals, the church may perform a role in helping to regulate and normalise grief in our Western postmodern culture. Otherwise, society currently lacks the means by which to inform the bereaved of what a normal range of feelings and behaviours may be following the death of a loved one. However, it is not just specifically while working with the bereaved to create meaningful funerals that the church can play an increasingly important role in enabling society to acknowledge death and personal mortality as part of life. For the church is a worshipping community which on a weekly basis marks the impact of death and endings on those still living, as well as the difficulty of waiting and living with the uncertainty and chaos that death brings and possibilities of new life for the deceased and those who mourn. Through working together with the bereaved and listening to their needs, feelings and experiences the church is reminded of the significance that she is a body which acknowledges the reality and pain of death and has a tradition of articulating lament and staying with suffering before celebrating and giving thanks for new life. The church is a living community, whose central narrative involves death, living through and articulating the desolation and isolation experienced and then hope. Her worship and witness is informed by all three elements of the Easter story and not simply by resurrection. Such are the prophetic possibilities for the church in the twenty-first century – to act as a counter to the prevailing attitude that death is something to be avoided, bypassed and kept at arms length rather than owned. In living with and through death and bereavement, possibilities of new beginnings may be discovered.

Concluding Thoughts

In the postmodern era, where the church is considered an irrelevance by many, or at best to have a benign, non-malevolent influence on society, her main opportunity for contact with those not affiliated with local communities of faith is when church representatives are sought out to help with a funeral. For many overworked clergy such approaches are perceived as a burden rather than an opportunity. The conclusion of this book is that the church needs to support and encourage its ritual leaders to help revise this attitude. Time, energy, commitment and a degree of vulnerability are required to support the bereaved and help them to co-construct meaningful funerals for their deceased loved ones. The bereaved, when given the opportunity, want to share their experience of loss. Moreover, they have a deep need to try to find meaning in their situation and in their relationship with the deceased. If church representatives are willing to engage with their pain and particular story, the bereaved can and want to do theology. If ritual leaders seek to work with those who grieve and begin where they are in their life journey, taking seriously their stories rather than attempting to control the content and form of funerals by imposing an alien liturgy, there are opportunities for the bereaved to make deeper connections or re-connect with the Divine Story. Paul Deyner (1997, 201) puts it well:

> One option is to cut loose from a society that does not respect Christian belief and ministry. If the family want a wordly, sentimental, 'I did it my way' type of funeral, they must seek it elsewhere; but such an attitude alienates, in their hour of need, the very people whom the minister is called to serve. A minister unable to cope with the confusion of thought and feeling which afflicts and characterizes the human condition will end up ministering to no-one. For many clergy, a funeral provides an opportunity not for confrontation, but for the encouragement of the tentative to advance in their faith.

The importance of ritual in the lives of the bereaved is underlined by Yann Martel in his novel *Life of Pi* (2002, 285). Marcel describes the intimate relationship which develops between a Bengal tiger and an adolescent called Pi Patel who spend several months together in a lifeboat after being shipwrecked in the middle of the Atlantic Ocean. Pi describes his leave-taking of the tiger, which he has named Richard Parker, when the small boat finally reaches land.

> I wept like a small child. It was not because I was overcome at having survived my ordeal, though I was. Nor was it the presence of my brothers and sisters, though that too was very moving. I was weeping because Richard Parker had left me unceremoniously. What a terrible thing it is to botch a farewell. I am a person who believes in form, in the harmony of order. Where we can, we must give things a meaningful shape . . .. It's important in life to conclude things properly. Only then can you let go. Otherwise you are left with words you should have said but never did, and your heart is heavy with remorse.

Martel's reflections highlight not only the spiritual need of Pi to acknowledge the end of a unique relationship but also emphasises the gap which ritual can fill in meeting such needs. Such is the importance of ritual at a time of endings and new beginnings to help reduce unfinished business which can be carried with us. Moreover, such is the significance of ritual that it offers possibilities of meaning and order in times of distress. Perhaps, if Pi's leave-taking from his feline friend had been planned and Pi had had someone who could have offered him guidance, resources and time and space in which to reflect upon his relationship with Richard Parker, he might have constructed a relevant ritual to act out the significance of their relationship and mark its physical ending. In doing so, Pi may not only have found a suitable way of expressing his feelings but also found some meaning in the shared act. Perhaps too, he would have been left not only with a memory of their leave-taking but also with well-formed memories of their shared journey which would have sustained him in the uncertainty of the future that lay ahead.

8

Recommendations for Practice

Prior to Practice

Before engaging with the bereaved and seeking to construct and share in meaningful funerals with them, it may be helpful for us as church representatives to reflect theologically on the following:

1) Whom do we believe the funeral and its process of construction is for – the bereaved, the deceased or both?
2) To whom does a funeral belong? How will our understanding of who owns a funeral influence our approach to constructing one with a bereaved family?
3) How can a funeral and its mode of construction meet the spiritual, psychological, social and practical needs of the bereaved?
4) How will the love and mercy of God be conveyed to the bereaved and the deceased in the process of co-construction and during the funeral itself?
5) How will any funeral we share in or help to create meet our needs as:
   a) ritual leaders,
   b) as pastoral theologians who seek to have theological integrity in what we enact and embody, and
   c) as human beings?

Prior to sharing in ritual construction and marking, it may be helpful for us as ritual leaders to reflect on our own stories and what we bring to any encounter with the bereaved:

1) Our wounded and mortal selves

It may be useful to do a bereavement inventory of our own experience of losses in life and how we dealt with them before working with bereaved. To what extent have our own personal bereavements or wounds encouraged or forced us to begin to deal with our own mortality?

2) Our gifted selves

What are our gifts in relation to providing sensitive bereavement care? Do we possess the innate abilities which are required to relate to persons *in extremis*? Checking this out with trusted others might be worth doing.

3) Our believing selves

To what extent have we reflected on our own beliefs in relation to soteriology, eschatology, resurrection and what form it takes and the Communion of Saints? How do our own beliefs influence the funerals we share in?

4) Our limited selves

What is our particular role in helping the bereaved to arrange, co-create and share in meaningful funerals? What about our role in post-funeral bereavement care? How aware are we of the roles of other carers who are involved (or potentially may become involved) in supporting the bereaved, for example, friends and other members of the family, funeral directors, crematorium attendants, the bereaved's general practitioner and bereavement support available from the church and within the local community? How aware are we of current models and theories of bereavement and to what extent does this knowledge inform the manner in which we construct and lead funerals?

5) Our sexual selves

Our sexuality is not only related to the genital expression of our feelings for another, it is also about how we feel being in our bodies and how we relate in our bodies to others. Thus, our sexuality influences greatly as to how we feel about touch and ritual action. At a time of bereavement, many bereaved persons find comfort in appropriate touch – a hand on a shoulder, a hug, a kiss on the cheek. How do we feel about these actions – with a member of the opposite sex, the same sex and of different ages?

6) Our playful selves

How do we build in time to play as well as working with the bereaved and the other demands on our time as church workers? How do we feed and nourish our humanity?

7) Our spiritual selves

Our faith, our work, our play and our relationships may be sources of meaning and purpose in our lives or they may be sources of unease, even distress. Where do we take our spiritual concerns and to what extent do we find time to attend to our own spirituality? When do we pause to listen and hear the voices (and Voice) within and around us?

Bereaved parents in this study indicated the most important resource a church representative has in helping to meet others' spiritual needs is their personhood and way of being and relating. Therefore, of primary importance for us as ritual leaders who are seeking to create meaningful funerals is to maintain and nurture our humanity and spirituality. This cannot happen unless we make time to play and to be still a priority in the rhythm of our lives, as well work with a spiritual director and/ or supervisor.

Theological Reflection

Periodically or after a particularly difficult funeral, it is of benefit to take time to reflect theologically on what we have been sharing in, preferably with a trusted other (a supervisor or mentor) or others. How have the stories, actions, grief and responses of the bereaved touched us as human beings and as ritual leaders? What have we found out about ourselves in relation to the seven categories outlined above? What have we learnt about how to care for the bereaved and how best to co-construct and share in funerals with them? And what have we learnt about God – has our understanding of theological issues been challenged, changed or affirmed in our practice? Crucially, what have we discovered about ourselves, about our way of caring and about how God informs the manner in which we co-create and share in our next funeral?

Principles of Practice

1) Knowledge of funeral practices and support
The ritual leader should acquaint herself with local funeral practices and what support is available for the bereaved.

2) Each funeral is unique
Although a basic structure for a funeral, informed by the ritual leader's tradition, may be a starting point for what is co-constructed, any funeral shared in is not merely an adaptation of a set liturgy. Each funeral is a one-off, not only in its content but also in its performance.

3) Make resources available
Create a portfolio of resources, sacred and secular, from which the bereaved might choose to help them own the funeral as well as helping to normalise grief.

4) Ensure consistency of practice
The development and use of a prompt sheet to ensure a ritual leader covers all areas (in relation to spiritual, psychological, social and practical aspects) involved in helping the bereaved to co-create and share in meaningful funerals is helpful.[1]

5) Clarify expectations
As ritual leaders we should ask when meeting for the first time with a bereaved family about a funeral, what it is that they envisage the funeral for their loved one will be like, what they want included in the funeral and what they would find unhelpful. Likewise, we should also outline our approach to constructing funerals and how they are performed; who we

---

1 An example of such a sheet to prompt discussion on various aspects of funerals and aid recording of a family's particular details, choices and beliefs can be found in appendix 1.

feel has ownership of the funeral and what the essential components of a funeral are for us (those things, if any, which are non-negotiable from our point of view). In encouraging such honest sharing about expectations it enables both the family and church representative to decide whether it is appropriate they continue working together or whether the family should look elsewhere for support which is relevant to their needs. The ritual leader may well be able to refer them to a colleague or another body who may be able to respond appropriately.

6) Offer active participation but never impose

The bereaved should never be made to feel that they have failed if they do not wish to co-author a funeral. The offer should be given but in the end the choice is theirs. They may wish to only help in co-construction to a certain degree, for example, share something of their loved one's story and choose a hymn but leave any readings or choice of music to the ritual leader and crematorium organist.

Neither should the bereaved feel pressurised to participate in a way they feel uncomfortable with during the funeral itself. To read something during the funeral, to help carry their loved one's coffin or to stand at the crematorium door afterwards, for example, are possibilities for participation but not cultural norms to be complied with.

7) Highlight importance of ritual action

Whilst constructing meaningful funerals it is important to help the bereaved reflect on the possible significance of ritual action as well as words to be said, music to be played and silence to be shared.

8) Co-construction is a process not an event

The co-creation of a funeral is an evolving process over a period. The bereaved should be encouraged to take their time in decision-making; for what is shared at a funeral cannot be undone. The bereaved should be assured that they could change their mind about decisions that they make, where practicable.

9) Talk through practicalities

Ensure the bereaved are comfortable with practicalities relating to the funeral as well as its contents and order. Do not assume that the bereaved will know what happens before, during or after a graveside or crematorium ceremony but offer to take them through what will normally happen, pointing out what choices they have (and the implications of making them). For example, what happens when they arrive at the crematorium, where will their loved one's coffin be during the funeral and when it will be lowered down for cremation.

10) The funeral is only one of many potentially healing ritual moments

It is not just the funeral that may ritually help meet the bereaved's spiritual needs following a significant bereavement. The ongoing process of the ritualisation of their loved one's life and death prior to, and after, the funeral is also potentially therapeutic for the bereaved; moments of creating and performing a variety of individual and shared meaningful ritual actions.[2] Discussion of appropriate ongoing modes of ritual remembering may be helpful for individuals and families.

11) The significance of incarnation

Being human, being ourselves as representatives of Christ, in our relating to the bereaved, during both co-construction and sharing in funerals, enables them to be themselves too and more likely to express themselves openly and honestly. The bereaved approach us to help with ritual marking due to our perceived ritual authority. However, in working with us, it is human warmth, compassion and availability that they appreciate and need, not a ritual leader utilising power to act out a detached role or impose an incomprehensible language or seemingly irrelevant narrative.

---

2 Bolton and Camp (1986–7) suggest that the bereaved may potentially benefit from caring professionals encouraging them to utilise ritual action as a means of dealing with their grief following their loved one's funeral.

In short, church representatives sharing in the co-construction and performance of meaningful funerals with the bereaved in the postmodern world is not so much about proclaiming the Gospel but about incarnating it. Graham (2002, 203) puts it this way:

> A commitment to the contextual and situated nature of human experience, if taken seriously by pastoral theology, therefore means that the only vocabulary available to Christian communities in articulating their truth-claims is that of pastoral practice itself. In their relationships and actions of care, social change, adult formation, worship and stewardship, communities of faith enact their core values of human being, truth, destiny, knowledge and obligation. The faith-community acts as the guardian of *practical wisdom* by which such purposeful action gains its authenticity and credibility, and serves as the medium by which truth-claims are forged and publicly articulated.

Embodiment of the Gospel according to Bennett Moore (2002, 14) relates not just to 'the incarnational but also the performative nature of theology'. Something of the Christian story of love and compassion is not only experienced by others in the personhood of the ritual leader but also in the manner by which she or he performs the funeral and relates to the bereaved before, during and after such ritual sharing.

Appendix 1

Checklist for Utilisation during Co-construction of a Funeral (to facilitate discussion and as an aide-memoir)

Beliefs of family
Involvement of family and friends
Readings/poems
Music in and out
Music during ritual
Hymns
Prayers
Blessing
Committal
Retiring collection
Order of service – typed (to be handed to those attending at door of crematorium/church)
Contact with crematorium – music/hymns/collection
Contact with funeral directors – retiring collection/music

Appendix 2

Demographic Characteristics of Parents Who Participated in the Interviews Performed

Interview number	Depr cat[1]	Funeral: religious or non-religious	Gestation of baby	Age of parent	Religious affiliation as child	Religious affiliation as adult
1	4	Non-religious	20+/40	Mother 33 Father 31	C of E C of S	None
2	4	Religious	18/40	Mother 38	C of S	None
3	3	Religious	18/40	Mother 39 Father 45	Cong. C of S	Non-active C of S
4	4	Religious	22/40	Mother 35 Father 35	RC Protestant	None
5	6	Religious	Full term	Mother 31 Father 40	None	None
6	3	Religious	22/40	Mother 29 Father 27	Both C of S	Non-active RC None

Continued

7	1	Religious	19/40	Mother 31 Father 32	C of S RC	None Non-active RC
8	4	Religious	20+/40	Mother 45 Father 48	C of S Free Church	Both non-active C of S
9	3	Religious	16/40	Mother 35 Father 35	Both C of S	Both Non-active C of S
10	4	Religious	26/40	Mother 31 Father 33	None	None
11	1	Religious	25/40 twins	Mother 32 Father 35	RC C of S	RC None
12	4	Religious	22/40	Mother 31 Father 39	None	None
13	2	Religious	20+/40	Mother 42 Father 41	RC C of S	Non-active RC None

1 Deprivation category: during healthcare studies such categories are commonly used as indicators of levels of social deprivation within a particular area. The various categories used are linked to postcode areas and are listed on a scale from 1 to 7. The higher the numerical value of the deprivation category the higher the level of unemployment, overcrowding in households and the prevalence of occupants not having higher education qualifications in that postcode area. (Carstairs and Morris 1991)

Abbreviations

C of S – Church of Scotland
C of E – Church of England
RC – Roman Catholic
Cong. – Congregational
Free Church – Free Church of Scotland
Protestant – feels affiliated to the re-formed tradition but no denominational or church affiliation.

Appendix 3

Resources and Information for Ritual Leaders and the Bereaved

Resources to Aid the Co-construction of Funerals

Abraham, M. 2007. *When We Remember: Inspiration and Integrity for a Meaningful Funeral*. Mona Vale, New South Wales (Australia): Three Things Pty Ltd.

Astley, N. (ed.) 2003. *Do Not Go Gentle – Poems for Funerals*. Tarset, Northumberland: Bloodaxe Books.

Bell, J. and Maule, G. 2004. *When Grief is Raw*. Glasgow: Wild Goose Publications.

Brind, J. and Wilkinson, T. 2008. *Funerals, Memorials and Thanksgiving Services: Creative Ideas for Pastoral Liturgies*. Norwich: Canterbury Press.

Church of England, 2000. *Common Worship: Services and Prayers for the Church of England*. London: Church House Publishing.

Church of Scotland, 2005. *Church Hymnary* (4th edn). Norwich: Canterbury Press.

Church of Scotland, 1994. *Book of Common Order*. Edinburgh: St Andrew's Press.

Dominica, F. 1997. *Just My Reflection: Helping Parents to Do Things Their Way When Their Child Dies*. London: DLT.

Galloway, K. 1996. *The Pattern of Our Days – Liturgies and Resources for Worship*. Glasgow: Wild Goose Publications.

Gill, S. and Fox, J. 2004. *The Dead Good Funerals Book*. Ulverston, Cumbria: Engineers of the Imagination.

James, H. 2004. *A Fitting End: Making the Most of a Funeral*. Norwich: Canterbury Press.

Morrell, J. and Smith, S. 2007. *We Need to Talk about the Funeral*. Bedlinog.

Lamb, J. 1989. *Bittersweet. . . Hellogoodbye: a Resource in Planning Farewell Rituals When a Baby Dies*. St Charles, MO.: SHARE.

MacGregor, L. (ed.) 2005. *Lament: Scottish Poems for Funerals and Consolation*. Edinburgh: The Scottish Poetry Library.

Methodist Church, 1999. *The Methodist Worship Book*. Peterborough: Methodist Publishing House. Accent Press Limited.

Munro, E. 2000. *Readings for Remembrance: A Collection for Funerals and Memorial Services:* New York: Penguin Books USA.

Paterson, D. (ed.) 2004. *All the Poems You Need to Say Goodbye*. London: Picador.

Pierce, P. 2003. *Miscarriage and Stillbirth – the Changing Response.* Dublin: Veritas.

SANDS, 1995. *Pregnancy Loss and the Death of a Baby: Guidelines for Professionals.* London: SANDS.

Smith, F. 2006. *Arranging a Funeral: a Book of Resources.* London: SPCK.

Ward, H. and Wild, J. 1995. *Human Rites – Worship Resources for an Age of Change.* London: Mowbray.

Watson, J. 2004. *Poems and Readings for Funerals.* London: Penguin Books.

Wienrich, S. and Speyer, J. (eds) 2003. *The Natural Death Handbook* (4th edn). London: Rider.

Whitaker, A. (ed.) 1984. *All in the End is Harvest.* London: DLT.

Wolfelt, A. 2000. *Creating Meaningful Funeral Ceremonies: a Guide for Families.* Fort Collins, CO: Companion Press.

Websites Offering Information and Support for the Bereaved

Cruse Bereavement Care offers information and advice to the bereaved as well assupport and counselling. Education and information are also available for those supporting the bereaved.
http://www.crusebereavementcare.org.uk

Child Bereavement Trust (UK) offers information and support to families and training for caring professionals.
http://www.childbereavement.org

Center for Loss and Life Transition (Bereavement Resource Center: USA).
http://www.centerforloss.com

Centering Corporation (Grief Resources Center: USA)
http://www.centering.org

Compassionate Friends (UK) offer support and information to grieving parents and families.
http://www.tcf.org.uk

GriefWatch (Resources for Bereaved Families and Professional Carers: USA).
http://www.griefwatch.com

Griefnet.org: an (online) Community of Persons Dealing with Grief (includes opportunity to create virtual memorials: USA)
http://www.griefnet.org

Missyou: enables ongoing ritual remembering online, offering a menu of informal rituals to participate in either alone or with others (UK).
http://www.missyou.org.uk

Royal College of Psychiatrists (UK): a website that offers clear and helpful information about grieving and sources of support for the bereaved.

http://www.rcpsych.ac.uk/mentalhealthinformation/mentalhealthproblems/
bereavement.aspx

SANDS (UK) offers support and information to parents whose babies are
stillborn or who have died in the neonatal period.

http://www.uk-sands.org

SHARE (Pregnancy and Infant Loss and Support: USA).

http://www.nationalshareoffice.com

The Widowed and Young Foundation provides a social and support network
(including online) for those widowed under the age of 50.

http://www.wayfoundation.org.uk

Winston's Wish (UK) offers guidance and information to children and their
carers after a family member dies.

http://www.winstonswish.org.uk

Bibliography

Ainsworth-Smith, I. and Speck, P. 1999. *Letting Go: Caring for the Dying and Bereaved* (2nd edn). London: SPCK.

Aldridge, D. 2000. The Challenge of Creativity. In *Spiritual Dimensions of Pastoral Care*, edited by D. Willows and J. Swinton, 188–95. London: Jessica Kingsley.

Anderson, H. and Foley, E. 1998–9. Ritual and Narrative, Worship and Pastoral Care, and the Work of Pastoral Supervision, *Journal of Supervision and Ministry* 19: 13–24.

— 1998. *Mighty Stories, Dangerous Rituals: Weaving Together the Human and the Divine*. San Francisco, CA: Jossey-Bass.

Armstrong, K. 2006a. I Must Hope that Others Will One Day Be Spared my Mother's Fate, *The Guardian* March 25: 32.

— 2006b. Our Truth is just a Bit-Player in the Tragic Conflicted Whole, *The Guardian* August 26.

Arthacarya, 2005. Ritual and Loss. In *Buddhist Reflections on Death, Dying and Bereavement*, edited by M. Lewin, 35–40. Newport, Isle of Wight: Buddhist Hospice Trust.

Astley, N. (ed.) 2003. *Do Not Go Gentle: Poems for Funerals*. Tarset, Northumberland: Bloodaxe.

Au, W. and Cannon, N. 1995. *Urgings of the Heart*. New York: Paulist Press.

Ballard, P. 2005. Taking Leave: The 'Good Death' Today, *Contact: Practical Theology and Pastoral Care* 146: 46–51.

Bartel, M. 2004. What is Spiritual? What is Suffering? *The Journal of Pastoral Care and Counseling* 58(3): 187–201.

Bauman, Z. 1991. *Modernity and Ambivalence*. Ithaca, NY: Cornell University Press.

Bell, J. 2005. We Cannot Care for You the Way We Wanted. In *Church Hymnary* (4th edn). Norwich: Canterbury Press.

Bennett Moore, Z. 2002. *Introducing Feminist Perspectives on Pastoral Theology*. London: Sheffield Academic Press.

Bloomfield, I. 1978. Counselling and Consultation, *Contact* 60(3): 19–24.

Bolton, C. and Camp, D. 1986–7. Funeral Rituals and the Facilitation of Grief Work, *Omega* 17(4): 343–52.

Bonn-Storm, R. 1996. *The Incredible Woman: Listening to the Women's Silences in Pastoral Care and Counselling*. Nashville, TN: Abingdon Press.

Bibliography

Bosticco, C. and Thompson, T. 2005. Narratives and Story Telling in Coping with Grief and Bereavement, *Omega* 51(1): 1–16.

Bouwsma, W. 1998. Conclusion: Retrospect and Propsect. In *From Facing Death: Where Culture, Religion and Medicine Meet*, edited by H. Spiro, L. Wandel and M. Curren, 189–98. Yale: Yale University Press.

Bowlby, J. 1980. *Attachment and Loss. Vol. 3. Loss, Sadness and Depression.* London: Hogarth.

Bregman, L. 2004. Defining Spirituality: Multiple Uses and Murky Meanings of an Incredibly Popular Term, *The Journal of Pastoral Care and Counseling* 58(3): 157–67.

Brown, C. 2001. *The Death of Christian Britain.* London: Routledge

Bruce, S. 2003. The Demise of Christianity in Britain. In *Predicting Religion: Christian, Secular and Alternative Futures,* edited by G. Davie, P. Heelas and L. Woodhead, 53–63. Aldershot: Ashgate.

Brueggemmann, W. 1991. *Interpretation and Obedience.* Minneapolis, MN: Augsburg Fortress.

— 1986. The Costly Loss of Lament. *The Journal for the Study of the Old Testament* 36: 57–71.

Burns, R. 2005. Epitaph on My Own Friend. In *Lament: Scottish Poems for Funerals and Consolation,* edited by E. MacGregor, 39. Edinburgh: The Scottish Poetry Library.

Butler, C. 2002. *Postmodernism: A Very Short Introduction.* Oxford: Oxford University Press.

Campbell, A. 1986 *Rediscovering Pastoral Care* (2nd edn) London: DLT.

Capps, D. 1984. *Pastoral Care and Hermeneutics.* Minneapolis, MN: Fortress Press.

Carmichael, K. 1991. *Ceremony of Innocence: Tears, Power and Protest.* New York: St Martin's Press.

Carr, W. 1985. *Brief Encounters: Pastoral Ministry through the Occasional Offices.* London: SPCK.

Carroll, B. 2001. A Phenomenological Exploration of the Nature of Spirituality and Spiritual Care, *Mortality* 6(1): 81–98.

Carter, S. 1974 (2000). The Good Boy. In *The Two-way Clock.* London: Stainer and Bell.

Catholic Communications Office, 2003. Jesus Christ: The Bearer of the Water of Life. A Christian Reflection on the 'New Age'. <http://www.vatican.va/roman_curia/pontifical_councils/interelg/documents/rc_pc-interegl_doc_20030203_new-age_en.html

Church of Scotland, 2000. Report to the General Assembly of the Board of Ministry. In *Reports to the General Assembly*, 17/3-17/25. Edinburgh: Church of Scotland Board of Practice and Procedure.

Clark, D. 2002. Between Hope and Acceptance: the Medicalisation of Dying, *British Medical Journal* 324: 905–7.

Cobb, M. 2005. *The Hospital Chaplain's Handbook.* Norwich: Canterbury Press.

Cohen, L. 2006. *Book of Longing.* New York: HarperCollins.

Cole, A. Jr. 2005. Elegiac Poetry: A Pastoral Response with Complicated Grief, *Pastoral Psychology* 53(3): 189–206.

Cooper-White, P. 2004. *Shared Wisdom: Use of the Self in Pastoral Care and Counseling.* Minneapolis, MN: Fortress Press.

Cowdrey, E. 2006. In BBC Radio 2 Life 2 Live – Comments. www.bbc.co.uk/radio2/life2live/comments.shtml (accessed 29/03/2006)

Crighton Smith, I. 2005. On Looking at the Dead. In *Lament: Scottish Poems for Funerals and Consolation,* edited by E. MacGregor, 24–5. Edinburgh: The Scottish Poetry Library.

Davidson, R. 1983. *The Courage to Doubt.* London: SCM Press.

Davies, D. 1994. Introduction: Raising the Issues. In *Sacred Places,* edited by J. Holm with J. Bowker, 1–7. London: Pinter Publishers.

Denyer, P. 1997. Singing the Lord's Song in a Strange Land. *In Interpreting Death: Christian Theology and Pastoral Practice,* edited by P. Jupp and T. Rogers, 197–202. London: Cassell.

Deveney, C. 2006. Pomp and Circumstance, *Scotland on Sunday Spectrum,* November 12: 13–16.

Dickinson, E. 1999. There's been a Death . . . In *Time's Tiding: Greeting the Twenty-First Century,* edited by C. A. Duffy. London: Anvil Press Poetry Ltd.

Dominica, F. 1997. *Just My Reflection: Helping Parents to Do Things Their Way When Their Child Dies.* London: DLT.

Durston, D. 1990. Funeral Service in the Process of Grieving, *Bereavement Care* 9(2): 18–20.

Dutton, Y. and Zisook, S. 2005. Adaptation to Bereavement, *Death Studies* 29: 877–903.

Dylan, B. 1973. *Forever Young.* Ram's Horn Music.

Eisland, N. 1994. *The Disabled God.* Nashville, TN: Abingdon Press.

Eliot, T. S. 2001. Burnt Notion. In *Four Quartets.* London: Faber & Faber Ltd.

— 1964. Genesis. In *Collected Poems 1909–1935,* translation and commentary by J. Sperna Weiland. Amsterdam: de bezige bij.

Fischer, K. 1989. *Women at the Well: Feminist Perspectives on Spiritual Direction.* London: SPCK.

Forrester, D. 2005. *Theological Fragments: Explorations in Unsystematic Theology.* London: T&T Clark.

— 2000. *Truthful Action.* Edinburgh: T & T Clark.

Foskett, J. 1999. The Challenge and Promise of Pastoral Counselling. In *Clinical Counselling in Pastoral Settings,* edited by G. Lynch, 124–39. London: Routledge.

Foskett, J. and Lyall, D. 1988. *Helping the Helpers: Supervision and Pastoral Care.* London: SPCK.

Fowler, J. 1996. *Faithful Change – The Personal and Public Challenges of Postmodern Life.* Nashville, TN: Abingdon Press.

Fowler, J. 1995. *Stages of Faith – The Psychology of Human Development and the Quest for Meaning (reprint).* San Francisco, CA: Harper & Row.

Bibliography

Freud, S. 1957. Mourning and Melancholia. In *The Complete Psychological Works of Sigmund Freud: Standard Edition* Vol. 14, edited and translated by J. Stachey: 243–58. London: Hogarth Press (Original work published in 1917).

Froggatt, K. 1997. Signposts on a Journey: the Place of Ritual in Spiritual Care, *International Journal of Palliative Nursing* 3(1): 42–6.

Garrick, D. 1994. The Work of Witness in Psychotherapeutic Rituals of Grief, *Journal of Ritual Studies* 8(2): 85–113.

Gerkin, C. 1997. *An Introduction to Pastoral Care.* Nashville, TN: Abingdon Press.

— 1984. *The Living Human Document: Re-Visioning Pastoral Counseling in a Hermeneutical Mode.* Nashville, TN: Abingdon Press.

Gergen, K. 1991. *The Saturated Self.* New York: Basic Books.

Gonzalez-Crussi, F. 1993. *The Day of the Dead and other Mortal Reflections.* New York: Harcourt Brace.

Goodacre, N. 1983. Direction, Spiritual. In *A Dictionary of Christian Spirituality*, edited by G. Wakefield, 114–115. London: SCM Press.

Gordon, T. 2006. *New Journeys Now Begun: Learning on the Path of Grief and Loss.* Glasgow: Wild Goose Publications.

— 2004. A Current Theory of Loss and its Christian Expression, *Scottish Journal of Healthcare Chaplaincy* 7(2): 28–33.

Graham, E. 2002. *Transforming Practice: Practical Theology in an Age of Uncertainty.* Eugene, Oregon, OR: Wipf and Stock publishers.

Graham, B. 2001. *You Raise Me Up.* Norway and Ireland: Universal Music and Acorn Music.

— 2000. Truth or Dare? Sexuality, Liturgy and Pastoral Theology. In *Spiritual Dimensions of Pastoral Care*, edited by D. Willows and J. Swinton, 95–101. London: Jessica Kingsley.

Grant, E., Murray, S. A., Kendall, M., Boyd, K. and Tilley, S. and Ryan, D. 2004. Spiritual Issues and Needs: Perspectives from Patients with Advanced Cancer and Non-malignant Disease. A Qualitative Study, *Palliative and Supportive Care* 2(4): 371–8.

Greig, A. 2001. Stair. In *Into You.* Tarset, Northumberland: Bloodaxe.

Green, R. 1987. *Only Connect: Worship and Liturgy from the Perspective of Pastoral Care.* London: DLT.

Hammarskjold, D. 1966. *Markings* (2nd edn). Translated by W. H. Auden and L. Sjoberg. London: Faber and Faber.

Hart, T. 2005. Pastoral Counselling or Spiritual Direction: What's the Difference? *Presence* 11(2): 7–13.

Hawkins, P. and Shohet, R. 2002. *Supervision in the Helping Professions.* Buckingham: Open University Press.

Hay, D. and Hunt, K. 2000. *Understanding the Spirituality of People Who Don't Go to Church: a Report on the Findings of the Adults' Spirituality Project.* Nottingham: University of Nottingham.

Heelas, P. and Woodhead, L. 2005. *The Spiritual Revolution – Why Religion is giving way to Spirituality.* Oxford: Blackwell.

Bibliography

Herrick, V. and Mann, I. 1998. *Jesus Wept: Reflections on Vulnerability in Leadership*. London: DLT.

Higginson, I. and Addington–Hall, J. 2004. The Epidemiology of Death and Symptoms. In *Oxford Textbook of Palliative Medicine*, (3rd edn) edited by D. Doyle, G. Hanks, N. Cherny and K. Calman, 14–24. Oxford: Oxford University Press.

Hockey, J. 2001. *Changing Death Rituals*. In *Grief, Mourning and Death Ritual*, edited by J. Hockey, J. Katz and N. Small, 185–211. Buckingham: Open University Press.

Holloway, R. 2005. Introduction. In *Lament: Scottish Poems for Funerals and Consolation*, edited by E. MacGregor, 9–12. Edinburgh: The Scottish Poetry Library.

Horner, A. 2005. *A Picture with the Paint Still Wet*. Milton Keynes: Revaph Publications.

Hunt, K. 2003. The Spirituality of Non-churchgoers. In *Predicting Religion*, edited by G. Davie, P. Heelas and L. Woodhead, 159–69. Aldershot: Ashgate.

Illich, Ivan. 1976. *Limits to Medicine: the Expropriation of Health*. London: Marion Boyars.

Irvine, A. 1997. *Between Two Worlds*. London: Mowbray.

Jacobs M. 1988. The Use of Story in Pastoral Care (Part One: Hearing Stories), *Contact* 95: 14–21.

James, H. 2004. *A Fitting End: Making the Most of a Funeral*. Norwich: Canterbury Press.

Joanna Briggs Institute, 2006. *Literature Review on Bereavement and Bereavement Care: Executive Summary*. Aberdeen: Robert Gordon University.

Jones, L. 2007. The Psalms of Lament and the Transformation of Sorrow. *The Journal of Pastoral Care and Counseling* 61(1–2): 47–58.

Kelly, E. 2007. *Marking Short Lives: Constructing and Sharing Rituals Following Pregnancy Loss*. Oxford: Peter Lang.

Klass, D., Silvermann, P. and Nickman, S. 1996. *Continuing Bonds: New Understandings of Grief*. London: Taylor and Francis.

Kubler-Ross, K. 1969. *On Death and Dying*. New York: Macmillan.

Lawbaugh, W. 2005. Existential, Theological and Psychological Concepts of Death: a Personal Perspective, *The Journal of Pastoral Care and Counselling* 59(1–2): 17–27.

Leech, K. 1987. Spiritual Direction. In *A Dictionary of Pastoral Care*, edited by A. Campbell, 265–6. London: SPCK.

— 1977. *Soul Friend*. London: Sheldon Press.

Lindemann, E. 1944. Symptomatology and Management of Acute Grief, *American Journal of Psychiatry* 101: 141–8.

Littlewood, J. 1993. The Denial of Death and Rites of Passage in Contemporary Societies. In *The Sociology of Death*, edited by D. Clark, 69–84. Oxford: Blackwell.

Lyall, D. 2001. *Integrity of Pastoral Care*, London: SPCK.

Bibliography

— Pastoral Counselling in a Postmodern Context. In *Clinical Counselling in Pastoral Settings*, edited by A. Boyd and G. Lynch, 7–21. London: Routledge.

Lynch, G. and Willows, D. 2000. Telling Tales: the Narrative Dimension of Pastoral Care and Counselling. In *Spiritual Dimensions of Pastoral Care*, edited by D. Willows and J. Swinton, 181–7. London: Jessica Kingsley.

MacCaig, N. 2005. Praise of a Man. In *Poems of Norman MacCaig*. Edinburgh: Polygon.

MacCaig, N. 1993. Between Mountain and Sea. In *Collected Poems: A New Edition*. London: Chatto and Windus.

MacGregor, L. (ed.) 2005. *Lament: Scottish Poems for Funerals and Consolation*. Edinburgh: The Scottish Poetry Library.

Marcel, G. 1950. *The Mystery of Being*, Vol. 1. London: The Harvill Press.

Martel, Y. 2002. *Life of Pi*. Edinburgh: Cannongate.

McCarthy, M. 2000. Spirituality in a Post-Modern Era. In *The Blackwell Reader in Pastoral and Practical Theology*, edited by J. Woodward and S. Pattison, 192–206. Oxford: Blackwell.

McCullough, W. 1998. Witnessing Death versus Framing Death. In *From Facing Death: Where Culture, Religion and Medicine Meet*, edited by H. Spiro, L. Wandel and M. Curren, 189–98. Yale: Yale University Press.

McFadyen, A. 1990. *The Call to Personhood: a Christian Theory of the Individual in Social Relationships*. Cambridge: Cambridge University Press.

McGough, R. 2006a. I Am Not Sleeping. In *Selected Poems*. London: Penguin.

— 2006b. Sad Music. In *Selected Poems*. London: Penguin.

Miller-McLemore, B. 1996. The Living Human Web: Pastoral Theology at the Turn of the Century. In *Through the Eyes of Women: Insights for Pastoral Care*, edited by J. Moessner, 9–26. Minneapolis, MN: Ausburg-Fortress.

Milne, A. A. 1928. *The House at Pooh Corner*. London: Metheun & Co.

Mitchell, K. and Anderson, H. 1983. *All Our Losses, All Our Griefs: Resources for Pastoral Care*. Philadelphia, PA: The Westminster Press.

Money, S. 1997. *I'll Be Missing You*. Bad Boy Records.

Moore, A. and Levison, C. 2003. Chaplains' Perceptions of Supervision, *Scottish Journal of Healthcare Chaplaincy* 6(2): 16–20.

Morgan, J. 1993. The Existential Quest for Meaning. In *Death and Spirituality*, edited by K. Doka and J. Morgan, 3–9. Amityville, NY: Baywood Publishing Co.

Murray, D. 2002. *Faith in Hospices: Spiritual Care and the End of Life*. London: SPCK.

Muse, S. 2000. Keeping the Wellsprings of Ministry Clear, *Journal of Pastoral Care* 54(3): 253–62.

National Council for Palliative Care, 2005. *Focus on Care Homes*. London: National Council for Palliative Care.

Neimeyer, R. 2005. Grief, Loss and the Quest for Meaning: Narrative Contributions to Bereavement Care, *Bereavement Care* 25(2): 27–30.

Bibliography

Nelson, J. 1979. *Embodiment: an Approach to Sexuality and Christian Theology.* London: SPCK.

Newbigin, L. 1989. *The Gospel in a Pluralistic Society.* Grand Rapids, Michigan, MI: Eerdmans.

Nouwen, H. 1969 (1981). *Intimacy.* San Francisco, CA: Harper.

Office for National Statistics and General Register Office for Scotland, 2001. *Census.* National Statistics Website: www.statistics.gov.org

Opinion Research Business, 2000. *The Soul of Britain Survey.* London: Opinion Research Business.

Page, R. 2000. *God with Us – Synergy in the Church.* London: SCM Press.

Parkes, C. M. 1996. *Bereavement: Studies of Grief in Adult Life* (3rd edn). London: Penguin.

— 1990. Foreword. In *Funerals and How to Improve Them,* edited by T. Walter, vii–viii. London: Hodder and Stoughton.

— 1986. *Bereavement: Studies of Grief in Adult Life* (2nd edn). London: Tavistock.

— 1984. Introduction. In *All in the End is Harvest,* edited by A. Whitaker, *IX–XII.* London: DLT.

— 1972. *Bereavement: Studies of Grief in Adult Life.* London: Tavistock.

Pattison, S. 1998. *A Critique of Pastoral Care.* London: SCM Press.

Pembroke, 2004a. Trinity, Polyphony and Pastoral Relationships, *The Journal of Pastoral Care and Counseling* 58(4): 351–61.

— 2004b. *Working Relationships- Spirituality in Human Service and Organisational Life.* London: Jessica Kingsley.

— 2002. *The Art of Listening.* Grand Rapids, Michigan, MI: Eerdmans.

Preston, P. 2005. This Circus of Grief Has Nothing to Do with Best, *The Guardian* November 29: 28.

Quoist, M. 1986. *The Breath of Love.* Translated by N. Smith. Dublin: Gill and Macmillan.

Ramshaw, E. 1987. *Ritual and Pastoral Care.* Philadelphia, PA: Fortress Press.

Reid, C. and Reid, C.1988. Sunshine on Leith (from the album *Sunshine on Leith).* Warner Chappell Music Ltd.

Rogers, C. 1967. *On Becoming a Person: a Therapist's View of Psychotherapy.* London: Constable.

Romanoff, B. and Thompson, B. 2006. Meaning Construction in Palliative Care: the Use of Narrative, Ritual, and the Expressive Arts, *American Journal of Hospice and Palliative Care* 23(4): 309–16.

Rosen, M. 2002. Don't tell me I mourn too much. In *Poems and Readings for Funerals,* edited by J. Watson. London: Penguin Books.

Roth, P. 1998. *American Pastoral.* New York: Vintage Books.

Rumbold, B. 1986. *Helplessness and Hope.* London: SCM Press.

Rusbridger, A. 2005. Sir John's Passion, *The Guardian* G2 December 12: 13.

Rush, C. 2006. *To Travel Hopefully: Journal of a Death not Foretold.* London: Profile Books.

Bibliography

Sawchuk, D., O'Connor, T., Walsh-Bowers, R. and Hatzipantelis, M. 2007. Exploring Power and Gender Issues Emergent in an Institutional Workshop on Preventing Clergy Sexual Misconduct, *Pastoral Psychology* 54(4): 499–511.

Schon, D. 1983. *The Reflective Practitioner*. New York: Basic Books.

Scott, M. 2006. Strange Arrangement. In *Book of Lightening*. Puck Records Ltd.

Scott, T. 2000. Chaplaincy – a Resource of Christian Presence, *Scottish Journal of Healthcare Chaplaincy* 3(1): 15–19.

Scottish Executive, 2002. *Guidelines on Chaplaincy and Spiritual Care in the NHS in Scotland*. NHS HDL 76.

Sheppy, P. 2003. *Death, Liturgy and Ritual – Vol. 1*. Aldershot: Ashgate.

Shuchter, S. and Zisook, S. 1993. The Course of Normal Grief. In *Handbook of Bereavement: Theory, Research and Intervention*, edited by M. Stroebe, W. Stroebe and R. Hansson, 23–43. Cambridge: Cambridge University Press.

Silvermann, P. and Klass, D. 1996. Introduction: What's the Problem. In *Continuing Bonds: New Understandings of Grief*, edited by D. Klass, P. Silvermann and S, Nickman, 3–27. London: Taylor and Francis.

Sims, C. L. 1998. Toward a Postmodern Chaplaincy, *The Journal of Pastoral Care* 52(3): 249–259.

Smart, B. 1993. *Postmodernity*. London: Routledge.

Smith, A. 1982. *The Relational Self: Ethics and Therapy from a Black Perspective*. Nashville, TN: Abingdon Press.

Solle, D. 1997. In *How I Have Changed: Reflections on 30 Years of Ministry*, edited by J. Moltmann, 22–8. London: SCM.

Soutar, W. 2005. Song. In *Lament; Scottish Poems for Funerals and Consolation*, edited by E. MacGregor, 55. Edinburgh: The Scottish Poetry Library.

Speck, P. 1978. Easing the Pain and Grief of Stillbirth, *Nursing Mirror* 146: 38–41.

Stafford, W. 1993. Consolations. In *The Darkness Around Us: Selected Poems of William Stafford*. New York: HarperPerennial.

Stairs, J. 2000. *Listening for the Soul: Pastoral Care and Spiritual Direction*. Minneapolis, MN: Fortress Press.

Steinham, G. 2005. I'm a Hopeaholic. There's Nothing George Bush Can Do about It, *The Guardian* September 13: 28.

Steinke, P. 2006. Black Milk: Literary Resources for Learning Pastoral Care, *The Journal of Pastoral Care and Counselling* 60(4): 335–42.

Stevenson, A. 2003. The Minister. In *Do Not Go Gentle – Poems for Funerals*, edited by N. Astley, 57. Tarset, Northumberland: Bloodaxe Books.

Stoddart, E. 2006. The Cost of Floral Tributes, *Contact: Practical Theology and Pastoral Care* 149: 28–37.

Stoter, D. 1995. *Spiritual Aspects of Healthcare*. London: Mosby.

Streets, F. 1996. Bearing the Spirit Home. In *From Facing Death: Where Culture, Religion and Medicine Meet*, edited by H. Spiro, M. McCrea Curnen and L. Palmer Wandel, 180–3. New Haven, CT: Yale University Press.

Stroebe, M. and Schut, H. 1999. The Dual Process Model of Coping with Bereavement: Rationale and Description, *Death Studies* 23: 197–224.

Stuart, E. 1992. *Daring to Speak Love's Name: a Gay and Lesbian Prayer Book*. London: Hamish Hamilton.

Swinton, J. 2007. *Raging with Compassion: Pastoral Responses to the Problem of Evil*. Grand Rapids, Michigan, MI: Eerdmans.

Tacey, D. 2004. *The Spirituality Revolution: the Emergence of Contemporary Spirituality*. Hove: Brunner-Routledge.

Taylor, C. 1991. *The Ethics of Authenticity*. Cambridge, MA: Harvard University Press.

The Clash, 1982. Should I Stay or Should I Go? In *Clash on Broadway*. Nineden Ltd.

The Guardian Editorial, 2005. In Praise of . . . Applause, *The Guardian* November 29: 30.

Thomas, E. 1987. Lights Out. In *The Oxford Book of Death*, edited by D. Enright. Oxford: Oxford University Press.

Thorne, B.1991. *Person-Centred Counselling: Therapeutic and Spiritual Dimensions*. London: Whirr Publishers.

van Gennep, A. 1960. *The Rites of Passage*. London: Routledge and Kegan Paul.

van Katwyk, P. 2002. Pastoral Counseling as a Spiritual Practice: an Exercise in a Theology of Spirituality, *The Journal of Pastoral Care and Counseling* 56(2): 109–119.

van Tongeren, L. 2004. Individualizing Ritual: the Personal Dimension in Funeral Liturgy, *Worship* 78(2): 117–38.

Wallbank, S. 1984. Death Makes Philosophers of Us All. In *All in the End is Harvest*, edited by A. Whitaker, 12. London: DLT in association with Cruse.

All Walter, T. 1999. *On Bereavement: the Culture of Grief*. Maidenhead: Open University Press.

— 1996. A New Model of Grief: Bereavement and Bibliography, *Mortality* 1(1): 7–25.

— 1994. *The Revival of Death*, London: Routledge.

— 1990. *Funerals and How to Improve Them*. London: Hodder and Stoughton.

Ward, F. 2005. *Lifelong Learning: Theological Education and Supervision*. London: SCM Press.

Webster, A. 2004–5. Bad Karma, *Living Spirituality News*. Winter: 2–3.

— 2002. *Wellbeing*. London: SCM Press.

Weick, K. 1995. *Sensemaking in Organisations*. Thousand Oaks, CA: Sage.

Welch, S. 1990. *A Feminist Ethic of Risk*. Minneapolis, MN: Ausburg Fortress.

Wells, S. 2007. *Power and Passion: Six Characters in Search of Resurrection*. Grand Rapids, Michigan, MI: Zondervan.

White, V. 2002. *Identity*. London: SCM Press.

Wierich, S. and Speyer, J. (eds) 2003. *The Natural Death Handbook* (4th edn). London: Rider and Co.

Bibliography

Willows, D. and Swinton, J. 2000. Introduction. In *Spiritual Dimensions of Pastoral Care*, edited by D. Willows and J. Swinton, 11–16. London: Jessica Kingsley.

Wood, J. 2003. *The Book against God*. New York: Farrar, Straus and Giroux.

Woodhead, L., Heelas, P. and Davie, G. 2003. Introduction. In *Predicting Religion: Christian, Secular and Alternative Futures*, edited by G. Davie, P. Heelas and L. Woodhead, 1–14. Aldershot: Ashgate.

Worden, J. W. 1991. *Grief Counselling and Grief Therapy* (3rd edn). New York: Springer.

Worden, J. W. 1983. *Grief Counselling and Grief Therapy*. London: Tavistock.

Wordsworth, W. 1990. A Pastoral Poem. In *The Oxford Anthology of English Poetry*, edited by J. Wain. Oxford: Oxford University Press.

Worsley, C. 1994. In Some foreign Tongue: the ASB Funeral Liturgy and the Bereaved, *Contact: the Interdisciplinary Journal of Pastoral Studies* 115: 23–29.

Wraight, H. and Brierley, P. (eds) 1999. *UK Christian Handbook 2000/01. Millennium Edition*. London: Christian Research/Harper Collins Religious.

All biblical quotations are from *The Revised English Bible* unless stated.

The Revised English Bible. 1989. Oxford and Cambridge: Oxford and Cambridge University Press.

Revised Standard Bible. 1952. Edinburgh: Thomas Nelson and Sons.

Index